source 34

2 **EDITORIAL**

3 **NEWS**
New galleries, prizes
Sam Coates

4 **PHOTOGRAPHY ON THE GETAWAY**
Sam Coates

8 **CURFEW**
Tobias Zielony

15 **ENGLAND MADE ME**
Clayton Irwin

23 **CLASSIFIED SUBJECTS**
Pete James

28 **A TEMPORARY CUSTODIAN**
Michael Wilson interview

32 **HOLDING ON**
Andrew Robinson

38 **REVISIONISTS TAKE NOTE**
Sean Sexton interview

44 **A NEW BLUE CARPET**
Stephen McCoy

EXHIBITION REVIEWS

48 **PSYCHO-GEOGRAPHY**
Roy Exley

50 **JOEL STERNFIELD**
Alicia Miller

52 **DAVID GOLDBLATT**
Mark Durden

54 **MARIO GIACOMELLI**
Martin Murray

56 **PETTER BOBBY**
Jane Fletcher

58 **SHARON YA'ARI**
Paul Tebbs

BOOK REVIEWS

60 **SPECTRAL EVIDENCE**
John Taylor

61 **ALEXEY BRODOVITCH**
David Campany

63 **THE IRISH, PHOTOGRAPHY IN IRELAND, A CENTURY IN FOCUS**
Justin Carville

65 **ACTUAL LIFE**
Richard West

66 **HOME**
Paul Tebbs

67 **OTT'S SNEEZE**
Roberta McGrath

69 **ENVISIONING SCIENCE**

69 **APERTURE AT 50**
David Brittain

source 34

SPRING 2003

Editors — John Duncan / Richard West
Web Editor — Stephen Hull
Design — Richard West / Keith Connolly
Front cover image — Tobias Zielony
Printing — W & G Baird

source PO Box 352, Belfast, BT1 2WB.
tel/fax: +44 02890 329691
info@source.ie http://www.source.ie

SOURCE IS PUBLISHED BY PHOTO WORKS NORTH IN CO-OPERATION WITH THE GALLERY OF PHOTOGRAPHY.

IT IS AVAILABLE IN IRELAND, THE UK, EUROPE, USA, CANADA, JAPAN, AUSTRALIA, NEW ZEALAND, SWEDEN. NEWSTRADE THROUGH COMAG, GALLERIES THROUGH CENTRAL BOOKSHOP/GALLERY RETAIL IN USA- BERNHARD DEBOER INC.

© NO PART OF THIS PUBLICATION MAY BE REPRINTED WITHOUT PERMISSION. THE VIEWS EXPRESSED IN SOURCE ARE NOT NECESSARILY THOSE OF THE PUBLISHERS OR EDITORS.

W9-CSL-835

GETTING YOUR WORK IN SOURCE

Source magazine is interested in seeing previously unpublished work for consideration for publication and wants to meet directly with photographers and artists. The following organisations will be facilitating these meetings on the dates listed. To arrange a time please phone 028 90329691 (from the ROI 048)or email john@source.ie

Friday 11th April, **Stills Gallery**
23 Cockburn Street Edinburgh

Saturday 12 April **Street Level**
26 King Street Glasgow

Friday 9th May **Gallery of Photography**
Meeting House Square Dublin

Saturday 10th May **Source**
3-10 Bridge Street, Belfast BT1

Thursday 15th May **Watershed**
1 Canons Road, Bristol

Sunday 18th May **Ffotogallery**
Chapter, Market Road, Cardiff

If you are unable to attend on these dates Source welcomes the submission of material for consideration for publication from artists and photographers working in Ireland or Britain. Work should be sent as small prints (10x8 photographic or inkjet) slides, or small scans on CD. Work can only be returned if accompanied by return postage and re-useable packaging. (We recommend the use of a photographic paper box)

Source will be holding its **A.G.M.** at 6.00pm on Wednesday 23th April at The Duke of York, Donegall Street, Belfast. The meeting is open to all subscribers. The agenda is as follows: minutes previous AGM, reports on years activities, finance report, election of new committee. If you wish to add to the agenda please do so in writing to Source before the 14th April.

COLLECTORS AND CURFEWS

The production of the computer game *Getaway* involved the recreation of central London using photography as its principal tool. Sam Coates the lead artist on the project explains how this was achieved. The way the images were cleaned and manipulated to be perceived in the game environment shows how the 'reality' of photographs can be used to contribute to the construction of a virtual world.

The reality of life in Britain is examined by Tobias Zielony and Clayton Irwin. In 2000 9pm curfews were introduced by the Blair government. The legislation covers those up to 16 years old. Tobias Zielony has photographed groups of teenagers in Bristol, Newport and Cwmbran as their curfew hour approaches and then passes. He follows them as they move towards the edges of these towns and away from the constraints of social control. Clayton Irwin's images are part of an ongoing project in which he tries to make sense of the political undercurrents in contemporary Britain. He has photographed racist attacks, suburbia and the celebration of the Queen Mother's 100th birthday.

Private collectors have an influence on the way we understand photography by simply bringing their collections together and more subtly by the uses and interpretations they give them. Sean Sexton has been collecting Irish photographs since 1973 and has strong views about what they can tell us about Irish history. Michael Wilson has a wealth of 19th century photographs which he would like us to consider in aesthetic terms. He also believes that the collector has a positive contribution to make to the national photographic institutions and that this has not been properly recognised in Britain.

An extreme impulse to collect is revealed by Andrew Robinson in his photographs of the home of a person with Obsessive Compulsive Disorder. He was asked to record it by the owner before it was forcibly cleared by the local council. On a smaller scale Stephen McCoy photographs the contents of his Dyson vacuum cleaner. These show strata that contain a dust archaeology of recent events in his house.

Libraries have an important and overlooked role in defining the way we understand photography, both in selecting what is purchased on behalf of the public but then also in deciding how it is categorised. Pete James discusses some of the dilemmas that face librarians when trying to fit this protean subject in their indexes.

This spring Source will be visiting more venues and meeting more photographers than ever, to bring you the best previously unpublished work. Finally, find enclosed the latest in Joachim Shmid's *Masterpieces of Photography* gaming card series, this issue it's the Americans.

The Editors

Conference

Following on from 'Photography/Philosophy/Technology' at the University of Brighton (see *Source* 31). Photo Forum, is organising a second conference *Sitting the Photograph* at the V&A on 9th and 10th May. Paul Tebbs, reviewing the previous event noted that there was more theoretical than practical insight, this time practitioners of different kinds are well represented and include the curators Val Williams and Jeremy Millar and the photographers Susan Meiselas, Martin Parr and Sophie Ristelhueber.

A week later on the 16th and 17th March the conference enthusiast can go to Chapter in Cardiff for *The Possibility of Seeing, The Artist, Photography and the Representation of Conflict*. At this event there will be of an emphasis on photographers with speakers including Willie Doherty, John Kippen and Susan Meiselas.

Prizes

The 2002 Kraszna-Krausz award for the best books on photography were won by *The Photographic Art of William Henry Fox Talbot* by Larry J Schaaf and *The Beautiful and the Damned* by Peter Hamilton & Roger Hargreaves. In the Autumn 2001 issue of *Source* the second book was commended as a 'well-documented introduction to 19th century photographic portraiture.' The publisher of each book wins £5,000.

There was no consensus among critics over who would win this year's Citibank prize. Simon Norfolk was the 'outstanding contender' for the *The Times*, while *The Guardian* (the show's official media sponsor) said he 'put you in touch with the roots of violence' but tipped the eventual winner Juergen Teller for the prize, Adrian Searle asked 'He does not appear committed to anything; he is neither worthy nor well-meaning. How can Teller not win the prize?' Encouragement for the runners up came unexpectedly in the shape of an article in the *Observer* 'Cash' section, John Wilson wrote, 'The reputation-making Photographers' Gallery in London is showing the shortlist of four in the UK's biggest photography competition. It's all part of creating new names. Is there a future Gursky, Dijkstra, Mikhailov or Billingham among this year's Citibank finalists?'

Pure Photography

In 1982 the then director of the Tate Gallery Alan Bowness explained that the Tate would not collect photography. Anyone who has been waiting for the last 21 years for photography to get into the Tate will now get three photography exhibitions all at once. In May Tate Liverpool is showing a Thomas Ruff retrospective, on 5th June Tate Britain will put on a large Wolfgang Tillmans show, including new work made in London. Finally on 6th June the Godzilla of Britain's art institutions Tate Modern will open *Cruel and Tender, The Real in 20th Century Photography*. According to the Tate website this show will include 'over twenty of the most important photographers working in the documentary style including; Robert Adams, Diane Arbus, Bernd and Hilla Becher... Described by some as 'pure' photography, this work is characterised by a sense of disengagement; it is analytical and descriptive in its approach to society and the landscape. At the same time, this kind of photography also demonstrates a concern for the subject matter.'

New Galleries

The National Museum in Bradford will be opening a new gallery specifically for photography in the Autumn of this year. It will be over 200 square metres and will show four exhibitions a year of work from its collection and by 'emerging contemporary photographers.' In addition to this the Museum also has longer term plans to open a gallery in London to give the museum a greater presence in the capital. Meanwhile The Photographer's Gallery's announcement of its planned move to a new London space is eagerly anticipated. They promise to provide a 'centre of photography in Britain, with increased exhibition space, a wider range of activities and innovative educational facilities.' A potential candidate for the new venue is thought to be disused tram terminus at Kingsway most recently used as an underground bunker in the film of the Avengers.

New 'zines

From time to time we receive new fledgling photography magazines and newsletters. December saw the first issue of *Scottish Photography Notes*, an initiative started by 'free and creative spirits who practice photography in Scotland.' The organisaton intends to run events such as talks and workshops and publish two issues of their *Notes* a year, a subscription is a very reasonable £6.00. Email sandesharpe@compuserve.com for more information.

A rather more enigmatic publication called *twostepsback* is by someone who signs themself 'cheers G'. G says that 'it's not just about things I've done... so just send in some stuff and it'll go in the next one, please just send me anything.' twostepsback@talk21.com

The new Photographer's Gallery?

SAM COATES

PHOTOGRAPHY ON THE GETAWAY

Ever since computer games moved into the third dimension and quite probably long before, game artists and programmers have been striving to create realistic and entirely believable images to draw players into the worlds they have created.

The game buying public's expectations have grown to the point where the virtual re-creations of real-life locations and characters are seen as essential seals of quality, especially for sports and racing titles. Cars, racetracks, sports stadiums, golf courses, household name sports stars and even famous actors have all been digitally captured and given to the gaming public to enjoy. This extends even to the movement of the characters themselves; it is now unimaginable that any top-ten sports title will not feature animation recorded directly from one of the top athletes in that sport via systems known collectively as motion-capture. Games endorsed by and bearing the names of such stars in their titles fill the shelves of games stores.

In such genres, game consumers now see reality as the leading artistic goal, whilst their gaming values insist that this does not get in the way of the game as a whole being FUN to play. This puts incredible pressure on game developers to stay ahead of their competition and provide the most accurate and recognisable models in the market place.

The Getaway is a self-styled gangster epic building on a long history of London gangster flicks and with cinematic ambition at its core. This ambition fed directly into the creative decision to avoid such gaming conventions as a score, two dimensional overlays of information cluttering the screen, spinning medical packs, pick-ups and the like. The art direction in general called for a game as good to watch as it was to play, and for the artwork itself, to be as near as technically possible, to reality. The backdrop to the action brought into being the largest ever recreation of a genuine location, the city of London, ever seen in a computer game.

The gameplay itself breaks down into two main components, driving around the city, which includes high-speed chases with rival gangs, stealing cars, avoiding the police *et al* and on-foot missions through interior locations as diverse as warehouses stuffed with stolen and counterfeit goods, a Soho lap-dancing bar and the now infamous assassination of a corrupt police officer inside his own station. From the player's point of view, the interiors allow them to engage in a variety of stealth and shooting missions while the game engine flows seamlessly from interior to exterior sections without any apparent loading or breaks in the action.

Obviously, with reality being both the source of the reference material for the game and the benchmark by which the visuals of *The Getaway* were judged, photography was one of the most important tools in the game's development. Digital cameras were used to create every single model in *The Getaway* and, like most games, these can be broken down into three main categories –

inanimate objects, in this case cars, guns and the like; animate objects, in the case of *The Getaway*, almost exclusively human characters; and the scenery/sets, the fabric of London and the interior locations of the levels.

In the case of inanimate objects, photography was used as a modelling tool. That is not to say that it wasn't exceptionally valuable. It was primarily a way to capture and recreate the most accurate representation of a real-life object possible. Along with plans, technical drawings and actual physical measurements it let us create highly detailed and realistic models for extremely important elements in the game. This was, of course, the most simple use of photography on the game and least interesting in the terms of this piece.

By contrast, *The Getaway* characters were built using a white-light scanner. This was a much more technically driven process and used sequences of calibrated photographs to reconstruct a model by extracting depth information from a grid projected on the subject. *The Getaway* worked in partnership with scanning specialists, to improve and develop their commercial product and create a useful solution for animated human head models. This collaboration and the unique technical considerations of scanning animated models are worthy of a whole article to themselves and, although of great technical interest will not be taken any further here where I prefer to concentrate on the third body of work as the one where the most creative intervention was required.

It was in the building of the sets, the city model and the interior gameplay locations that the game artists had the most latitude to use their creative skills. Having stressed the quest for reality and the emphasis on photography so far, this may well seem contradictory. What follows is an attempt to explain the process and the theory behind it. However, before we launch into that discussion, it will benefit the reader to have an understanding of the basic technology behind the

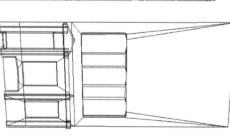

art and photography's place in its creation, the step-by-step process from camera to screen.

First of all the artist had to get out into the streets or the location and systematically photograph each surface from as flat and perspective free an angle as possible, making sure to include reference items for scale. As part of this survey, further reference photographs were also taken along with video footage and walkthroughs to allow the separate pictures to be reconstructed into entire scenes back in the studio. The biggest enemy here was the weather, whereas in traditional photography light is expressly used to pick out the form and modelling of an object, in *The Getaway* this was done by the in-game lighting and as neutral a starting point as possible was the goal. To that end we could not effectively shoot when the sun was shining as this would have left the artists with a huge amount of work to do to paint out shadows and colour correct the different faces of the buildings. There were similar problems on days when it had been raining, wet surfaces are generally darker and much more reflective than dry ones, and as buildings dry out they become patchy and stained. Luckily for the art team, London is generally an overcast and grey city and

waiting for the weather to change never cost us more than a 24 hour delay and there was always other work that could be done in the mean time. An extension of this problem was managing the surveys to avoid shooting tree-lined areas during spring or summer as foliage obscured the buildings.

Once back in the studio, the first step was to reconstruct the multiple images to build up a single building face. These were then perspective corrected, colour corrected and cleaned up. As can be seen in the accompanying images, this often involved a great deal of artist intervention to remove the unavoidable city noise that the original images contain. In the given example, railings, bicycles and black bags full of rubbish all had to be painted out by the artist to leave a clean image of the building fabric. The result is a flattened, ironed out image that can be converted into a 'texture map' and applied to a model.

The virtual geometry of *The Getaway* was constructed in industry standard 3D modelling software, as used in everything from the special effects business to industrial design. Models were relatively simple surfaces described by strips of polygons. Looking at the wireframe mesh in the entertainment product in the classic escapist mould, real to look at but much more fun than real life to play. The illusion of reality is there to draw the player in and suspend their disbelief, to place them in a game world that they can believe exists.

The first and obvious way in which the London in *The Getaway* deviated from reality was in its road layout. Although all roads in the game were straight from the genuine London street plan and were modelled extremely accurately, right down to their heights above sea level, they are a sub-set chosen from the whole of the A-Z for gameplay reasons and within a realistic workload for the artists involved in the construction. The removal of many, many streets also served several game design goals, it allowed the overall scale of the map to become larger, more varied and more accessible to the player. People generally wish to drive faster than in real life and in the process cover larger distances, they need to learn to navigate via landmarks and thinning out the road density allows them to learn more quickly and effectively.

The simple fact that many streets have been removed meant that a lot of filling in was required. This is where the creative input was required, each 'gap' had to be filled sympathetically. The overall image of the street

accompanying image shows just how simple these meshes were. Fine detail and visual interest was created by wrapping this simple model with a two dimensional image, almost like wall-papering, this 2D image is known as the 'texture map.'

All texture maps in *The Getaway* came from photographic sources and retouching without too much over-drawing and simplification was a real skill that the artist had to learn. It was not just a case of pointing a camera, removing the inherent perspective from the image and mapping the result to a model. Visual noise had to be removed and fine line work was particularly problematic. As models usually end up in a library and were re-used, it was important that the artist ironed-out the distinctive features that litter most buildings, everything from burglar alarms (generally bright yellow and distracting anyway) street numbers, graffiti and sometimes even the distinct patterns and stains in brick or stone work. It was important that the artist understood how the eye would perceive the end image and anything that would dominate it unnecessarily, either in colour or contrast, had to be removed/reduced. Windows were particularly troublesome in this area as they were often full of reflections of things that would not be present in the final game (often including the photographer themselves). Even such things as the inevitable backs of PC monitors needed to go as they resolved

to bright blocks of white noise that cluttered the end visuals. Textures also had to conform to art directions on colour as defined specifically for the game and be corrected following standard rules. The final results were neutralised maps that could be applied to the geometry to appear in the game. This is an increasingly common way of working for games artists.

In practical terms, all these considerations intertwine and blur and the simple answer to the simple question 'Is *The Getaway* an attempt at creating a completely real game?' is, of course, NO it most definitely is not. The long answer is that several million people live out their daily lives in London and have little to no exposure to criminal activity, high-speed chases and gun battles. It is first and foremost an

was to change as little as possible leaving no visual 'scars' that made it obvious that a street had been removed. In order to achieve the desired results, it was important for the art team to develop strong observation skills to interpret photographic material and build a vision of reality rather than an accurate recreation. In many ways building *The Getaway* was like impressionistic painting with polygonal models, the line of the street and distance from the road, the silhouette of the skyline, the general flavour of affluence or poverty, the proportion of grit and grime and the age and style of the architecture were far more important than accuracy and detailed recreation. To do this, it was essential for each and every artist to get out and about and physically walk the streets of London, to immerse themselves in the world they were building.

This process of observation and interpretation in order to build an artistically satisfying location which also meets gameplay goals, was taken much, much further in the Interior/On-foot sections of the game. For these, the artist was the true servant of the gameplay, which took absolute precedence and dictated the design, layout and dimensions of each space.

For the interiors, the gameplay rulebook was stringent and defined everything from the dimensions of doorways to how the character interacts with objects. In general these rules are almost all derived from the distances the character covers when animating through key-game moves. These rules allow the player to sneak the character along walls, lean out from corners, roll across doorways etc. Inevitably, real world interiors do not conform to such tight rules and the artists had to manipulate reality to conform whilst maintaining the original flavour of the location as surveyed. This worked in combination with the fact that no one real location truly matched the vision in the game designer's mind. The solution was again to draw on the creativity and sensibilities of the artist and have them build the locations up from an amalgamation of sources whilst retaining the consistency of vision. Again, all reference material was gathered from photographic sources and the elements carefully brought together to create the final locations as they appear in the game, examples of which appear here side-by-side with original reference photographs.

In conclusion, it would seem that realistic looking games are very much here to stay but that the visual language of games requires very careful use of that reality in order to create satisfying and fun play experiences. The main role of the game artist is to create believable locations, characters and objects that capture and hold the player's imagination. This applies equally whatever the art direction of a game. Be it cartoon graphics or photographic realism, the best game artwork must create its own reality with absolute consistency of visuals that communicate the design goals to the player. In many ways *The Getaway* has more in common with many fantasy titles, at least in terms of art direction, we both strive for a fidelity of image that is absolutely real, neither world truely exists, the action has never actually taken place but we strive to convince the player that, should they have been in the right place at the right time, they could have looked through the lens of a camera and taken the picture that appears on the screen.

CURFEW - A JOURNEY INTO THE NIGHT

TOBIAS ZIELONY

There was a time in my childhood when I had to return home when the streetlights were turned on. The young people I photographed in Bristol, Newport, and Cwmbran prefer to stay out later. Hanging around bus stops, street corners, shop fronts, car parks and wastelands at the edge of town, they wait for something to happen. Some of them however have got into trouble. It is only since the beginning of the year 2001 that the police have imposed curfews on individuals. James, Nathan, John, Craig, Lee, they all to have to be back home at nine o'clock p.m. and stay in all night with the police calling every so often to check if they accord to the curfew.

Curfews have been around for hundreds of years and were expected in cities that have been invaded. At the same time they served as a tool of control of Jews during the Third Reich and the black population in the United States during slavery and afterwards. The first curfews for young people in the US became popular in the early 1900s. During the late 1980s they started being enforced again and in May 1996 President Clinton announced that he was supporting a new teen curfew policy leading to a massive increase of weekday curfews at 9pm for teenagers. In 1998 the first curfews for under 10-year-olds were introduced in the UK and at the end of the year 2000 the legislation was expanded for under 16-year-olds.

At the time the street lights are turned on, my work Curfew begins a journey into the night of five housing estates in Bristol, Newport, and Cwmbran. Here like all over the country young people meet outside the houses in order to kill time. The increasing darkness indicates the approach of the curfew at 9pm and turns the meeting points into isolated islands inside an insecure territory. When moving in closer the photographs look into the young and often vulnerable faces of those who move further and further beyond the network of surveillance and social control.

CLAYTON IRWIN **ENGLAND MADE ME**

CLASSIFIED SUBJECTS

PETE JAMES
PHOTOGRAPHS BY ROY PETERS

PHOTOGRAPHY, PHOTOGRAPHS AND PUBLIC LIBRARIES

In recent times a growing body of work has begun to chart and re-assess the historical relationship between the photograph and institutions of knowledge: i.e. museums, libraries and archives. In some situations this work has resulted in the restructuring of the systems of classification, the physical relocation of collections and the development of new roles for the photograph within these domains. Writers and curators have also sought to develop new understandings of the history of books illustrated with original photographic prints and that of the history of the literature of photography. Together this work has helped to establish new understandings of the institutional, material and cultural history of photography: a history that goes beyond the simple canonical model of great pioneers and artists. This essay seeks to open up debates about a related, yet relatively unexplored field: that of public reference libraries and the resources they dedicate to representing photography, this being primarily expressed through issues such as the books that are purchased and the way they are catalogued and physically ordered within the institution. This is in itself a substantial subject area and one that cannot be fully understood in isolation from the related history of libraries and of photography. However, within the constraints of this essay it is not possible to do more than present some of the key questions relating to this subject. These questions will be addressed largely in reference to my own institution, Birmingham Central Library: one of the largest public reference libraries in Europe and home to one of the national collections of photography.

The most common definition of a library is 'a building or room containing a collection of books'. However, libraries come in all different shapes, sizes and specializations i.e. private or subscription libraries; national libraries; public libraries (lending and reference); academic libraries; art libraries; museum libraries and those of learned societies. Each serves a particular function and often a specific constituency of users. Public reference libraries were first established in Britain after the passing of the Public Libraries Act by Parliament in 1850. They were created to provide all classes of society with free access to books, journals and newspapers and were part of the same reform movement that sought to establish public museums and art galleries to enable the so-called 'elevation of the masses'. In many cases the intimate connection between the two was such that one was constructed or given space within the other. Most of the large metropolitan public libraries that exist today provide both reference and lending services. In so doing they strive to uphold the founding principle of free public access to their resources and issue 'customer service statements' which seek to explain not so much what they are as what they exist to do. My own institution for example 'exists to provide promote and encourage access to reading, information, lifelong learning, leisure and cultural activities for everyone.'

Public reference libraries and photography developed at a comparable historical moment during the first half of the nineteenth century. Indeed photography, public libraries, museums and art galleries were all part of a conjoined positivist enterprise: to collect, collate and published over a century apart. William Jerome Harrison's bibliography published in *The Photographic News* in 1886 contains some 340 entries. Laurent Roosens and Luc Salu's bibliography published in 1989 contains some 11,000 entries in more than a dozen languages arranged under some 3,000 subject headings and subheadings.

However, it is not simply the sheer number of publications that increased during this period, but also the type of publication. Perhaps the most significant development in this regard was the introduction of the half-tone process in the 1880s. Although the albumen print and photomechanical processes such as the Woodburytype made possible the production of a significant range of photographically illustrated books, it was the introduction of the half tone process – which enabled the transfer of the photographic image to the printing block – in the mid 1880s that truly revolutionised both the scope and scale for the publishing of books on photography and those illustrated with photographs. Within the specific realm of photographic literature it enabled publishers to navigate a shift away from the format of earlier publications comprised solely of text and those illustrated with 'engravings' made after original photographs or photomechanical reproductions. It made possible the production of new forms of illustrated photographic literature ranging from general and thematic histories of photography to monographs by and about individual practitioners.

Librarians seeking to collect, organise and make accessible the ever expanding variety of publications about photography and photographically illustrated books have always faced two key problems: firstly, the manner in which the process is considered simultaneously both an art and a science; and secondly, the plurality of discourses in which photography had participated. In order to help them position books in the right place on the shelves so as to make them easier for us/them to find, librarians most commonly use the Dewey Decimal System (DDS) which associates a number sequence with every field of knowledge. Within the DDS knowledge is divided into 10 fields and amongst these ten main classes The Arts are associated with the numbers in the 700s sequence. Each main class has ten sub-divisions and within this sequence Photography & Photographs are categorised in the 770s sequence. Further sub-divisions provide further numerical categories, for example: techniques, procedures, apparatus, and equipment (771); specific fields and special kinds of photography and related activities (778) and finally photographs (779). The current edition of the DDS (20/21) contains no less than eight pages devoted to the fields for classifying photography. As the term 'current edition' implies, the DDS is subject to periodic revision and items appearing in one class in one edition may subsequently be assigned to another in a later version. Just to complicate matters further, subjects such as

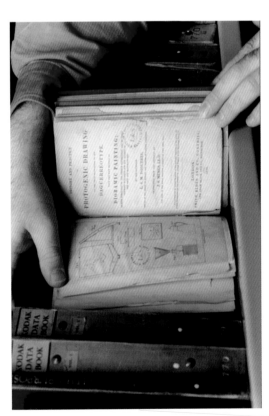

disseminate knowledge about the world so as to facilitate social progress. The figurative powers of photography and belief in its fidelity to nature led to its widespread use as a tool to aid the study of history, science, art, industry, topography and nature – both in terms of collecting and disseminating information. Photographs stored in albums and portfolios were thus placed into an already established system of storage and cataloguing developed for books, prints and drawings within the library. The potential for mass reproduction made possible by Talbot's negative/positive process also led to the widespread use of laid down photographs as illustrations in books and these were acquired in large numbers by libraries of all kinds after the introduction of the albumen print in 1851. These were also placed on the library's shelves in accordance with the existing systems of classification.

In addition to becoming an aid to learning, photography itself naturally became a subject of study. The desire for knowledge about the processes and equipment needed to make photographs was largely met through the production of technical literature and within three years of the announcement of Daguerre and Talbot's processes in 1839, no less than thirty-two technical manuals were published. Photography's rapid development led to the publication of more comprehensive works such as photographic dictionaries, encyclopaedias and historical accounts of the process and its various applications. Periodicals solely devoted to photography were not far behind, one of the earliest English publications being *The Liverpool Photographic Journal*, the forbear of *The British Journal of Photography*, first issued in 1854. From these early beginnings the rapid growth in the publication of photographic literature can perhaps best be gauged by comparing the entries in two bibliographies of photography photogrammetry and photomechanical reproduction can also be classified in sequences outside the 770s assigned for photography.

In seeking to place any given publication within this or other sequences within the DDS, the first question a librarian usually asks when confronted with a new book of photographs is: is the focus of the work on the artistic value or technical aspects of photography? In other words, does the work truly belong in the category of science or arts? If yes, the work belongs in the 700s sequence; if no – if the focus of the work for example is on the plight of the poor rather than the artistic qualities of the photographs or the equipment or processes associated with making the images – then the work is classed with the subject of the photographs. The DDS is of course subject to the interpretation of individual librarians, these interpretations change over time and anomalies occur as a natural part of this process. For example, Birmingham Library holds a copy of a 12-volume work *British Museum Collections* (1872) illustrated with over 900 original photographs. Each volume deals with the antiquities held in different departments, i.e Egyptian, Assyrian, Greek, Etruscan and British, etc. The strict application of the DDS means that the work is currently split between two subject information departments, Local Studies and History (3 volumes) and Arts, Language and Literature (9 volumes) with three different DDS class marks being used to classify the volumes. Elsewhere Fay Godwin's book *Landmarks* (1998) is classified under 'environmental photography' in the Science and Technology Department field of applied photography, and is found alongside books dealing with cameras, process and optics. Another work by the same artist, *Remains of Elmet, A Pennine Sequence, with Poems by Ted Hughes* (1979) is catalogued and held by The Arts, Language and

Literature Department.

Whilst this in itself may appear problematic, it is possibly made all the more so in Birmingham because books on photography are split between two subject information departments and these are located on separate floors of the building. However, it was not always so. Birmingham Library was originally broadly divided into two main areas: Humanities and Science and Technology. Within this structure books on photography were largely found in the Science and Technology section. In the 1970s a vogue for a broader range of subject information departments evolved within library practise. The adoption of these new structures in Birmingham saw the formation of a new Arts, Language and Literature Department, and within this new domain material from various parts of the library were drawn together into a subject area that dealt with photography as an art form within the context of the fine arts. These changes in themselves reflected a general growth in interest in photography for the 1970s was a period when photography became part of the world of museums, higher education, the art market and culture in general. This was marked at a national level by the Arts Council of Great Britain's formation of a Photography Committee (1971) and landmark exhibitions such as the Bill Brandt show at the Hayward Gallery (1969) and *From Today Painting is Dead*, shown at the V&A in 1972. These in turn prompted the appearance of numerous new books, exhibition catalogues and journals which sought to re-evaluate and re-place photography within the realms of the fine arts.

At the time of writing it was not possible to establish the extent to which the organisation of photography books and subject information departments in Birmingham Library exists in other institutions in the UK. However, there are undoubtedly other models of practice such as that

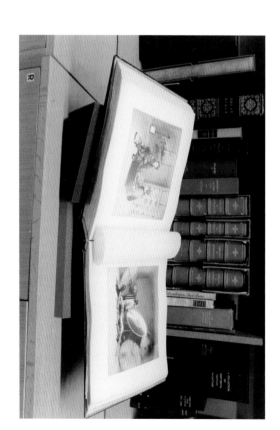

adopted at Finsbury Library. Here books and journals on all aspects of the subject were drawn together to form the Metropolitan Special Collection on Photography, the largest such collection in the South East. The collection is housed in a closed access store and access is generally made by appointment. The organisation of books and journals in this fashion raises yet another question: at what point does a library stop being a library and become a museum of books and journals?

This issue was taken up by Douglas Crimp in his 1993 essay 'The Museum's Old, the Library's New Subject'. Crimp describes how in the 1970s, Julia van Haften, a librarian in the Art and Architecture Division of the New York Public Library (NYPL), became interested in photography. In pursuit of this interest she discovered that 'the library itself owned many books containing vintage photographic prints' dispersed throughout its numerous thematic collections. She decided to organise an exhibition of photographs...because no-one had previously inventoried these materials under the single category of photography'. At the time she installed her exhibition 'photography's prices were beginning to sky-rocket' and books that previously were not deemed worthy of a place within the library's Rare Books Division were now worth a small fortune. Van Haften went on to create a new library division, that of Arts, Prints and Photographs to which she added photographs culled from all the other library departments. In so doing, the materials were 'reclassified according to their newly found value, the value that is now attached to the "artist" who made the photographs'. Crimp states that 'thus what was once housed in the Jewish Division under the classification "Jerusalem" will eventually be found in Arts, Prints and Photographs under the classification "Auguste Salzmann"'. He goes on to conclude that 'if photography was invented in 1839, it was only discovered in the 1960s and 1970s'.

Crimp's critical assessment of events in NYPL addresses understandable concerns about the typological re-classification and re-organisation of such materials. Furthermore, the issues he raises relating to books illustrated with original photographic prints are now equally applicable to the domain of early photographic literature, much of which could be assigned rare books status. Perhaps librarians have concerns that Crimp has not considered? For example, the free public access provided to rare and valuable volumes such as those he describes have always presented problems of theft and mutilation. The conflict between free public access, conservation and security are not easy to resolve, particularly within the limited resources available to most libraries. The advent of digital imaging and computer catalogues undoubtedly provides one solution by allowing the creation of digital surrogates so that a volume or image can exist and

function in two realms within the same institution simultaneously. This is the approach currently being adopted by The British Library where specialists are compiling a database (currently standing at some 5,000 entries) of works containing original photographs and texts relating to the development of photography and the early processes of the photo-mechanical production of books.

The example of the mis-classification (?) of Godwin's book cited earlier is perhaps symptomatic of another set of problems linked to the changing status of photographs and photography since the 1970s. In the early part of that decade photographers like Paul Hill began making work that addressed debates about photography as an autonomous means of self-expression. Whilst Hill and his contemporaries drew upon nature for their subject matter, they were creating images, sequences and photo essays that sought to go beyond the forms of documentary practise that dominated photography in the 1960s and make work that operated on the level of metaphors: photography as art. In his 1993 essay, Crimp gives an example of how one photographic book presented problems for the librarian at NYPL. He recalled that when hired to do picture research about the history of transportation he found himself browsing through their stacks where he came across a copy of the book *Twentysix Gasoline Stations* (1963) by Ed Ruscha. Crimp recalled thinking 'how funny it was that the book had been mis-catalogued and placed alongside books about automobiles', because he knew 'as evidently the librarians did not, that Ruscha's book was a work of art and therefore belonged in the art division.' Crimp subsequently changed his mind and concluded that Ruscha book made 'no sense in relation to the categories of art according to which books are catalogued in the library.' For him, the fact that there was nowhere for this work 'within the present system of classification' was 'an index of the books radicalism with respect to established modes of thought'. Unfortunately Crimp's interesting observation gives little comfort to the poor librarian seeking to place such works within the existing systems of classification. The more recent advent of 'artists using photography' perhaps serves to complicate the matter even further. One only has to think of the manner in which many commentators (mis)located Richard Billingham's work *Ray's A Laugh* (1996) within the realm of documentary practise to understand the potential problems for the librarian or cataloguer.

Problems relating to the question of 'who' and therefore 'how' such books are selected and catalogued are one of many points raised by Amanda Duffy in her essay 'Visual Arts Provision in Public Libraries: Threats and Opportunities (*Arts Libraries Journal* 1999)'. Duffy suggests that the loss of knowledge and expertise caused by cuts in the number of specialist arts posts in public libraries, the replacement of these posts with 'the so-called generic librarian' and increased reliance 'on non-professional staff to answer enquiries and, in some cases, to select stock', may cause problems in the future. Given the range and number of publications on photography now produced every year, an interest in the subject seems a minimum requirement for anyone asked to select stock from the publishers lists supplied to public libraries by the likes of Photoworks and Dewi Lewis Publishing.

Another key factor in the decision making process is that of resources – for resources read dwindling library budgets. In a world of limited resources the increasing costs of some photography publications – as opposed to those of popular fiction titles, travel books or children's literature, etc – can lead to questions of priorities. Why buy one expensive monograph when the same amount of money can buy three, possibly four other titles?

The matter of free public access and censorship has also proved a re-current problem for librarians in relation to some photographic literature. Loudly voiced concerns about the acquisition with public funds of photography books dealing with the body, sex and gay and lesbian photography, volumes deemed 'pornographic' by some, have raised many issues. Librarians have faced similar issues with other forms of art books – particularly those dealing with human anatomy, the nude and erotic imagery. However, it could be argued that the increasingly graphic nature of the imagery in some more recent books and the widespread controversy caused by their publication has brought greater public and professional attention to this matter. In the past librarians adopted a variety of strategies for dealing with such issues. These included housing such works in a special locked bookcase in the chief librarian's office, and issuing this stock under the strict public scrutiny of a member of staff on the so-called

'desks of shame'. For many years in Birmingham, books such as Henry Mortenson's technical manual *Lighting the Nude* (1950), in which all the illustrations were subject to the tasteful touch of the air brush, were served under such conditions.

More recently the public controversy surrounding books such as Sally Mann's *Immediate Family* (1991), which included images of her children naked, and Madonna's steel bound volume *Sex* (1992), with photographs by Stephen Meisel of the singer and other models acting out sexual fantasies, undoubtedly caused many librarians to consider whether they should acquire and place such items on their shelves. Perhaps the most influential case was the raid carried out by members of the West Midlands Paedophile and Pornography Squad in the The Library of the University of Central England in 1998. The police confiscated a copy of the book *Mapplethorpe* (1992), declared parts of the book obscene, and placed the University's Vice Chancellor under threat of imprisonment unless he agreed to the destruction of portions of the book. This led to the withdrawal of all Mapplethorpe titles in many public libraries until the case was finally resolved.

Many issues relating to reference libraries and the resources they dedicate to representing photography remain to be identified and addressed. For example, do librarians place books on digital photography, the software associated with image management and desktop publishing with photography or computing? That, perhaps, is the subject for another essay altogether.

I would like to thank my colleagues Patrick Clarke and Norman King for their help in researching this article.

A TEMPORARY CUSTODIAN

MICHAEL WILSON TALKS TO RICHARD WEST. PORTRAIT BY GARETH MCCONNELL.

RW: Where were you born?

MW: I was born in New York city, raised in California, went to university as an engineer and then went to Stanford Law School. Worked as a lawyer first for the government and then for a private law firm. During the Vietnam war I was working on military contracts, then I got into tax and international business law, about 1974 I came to London. The two year leave of absense became permanent, I've been over here ever since.

RW: What did your parents do?

MW: My stepdad was a movie producer, came over in '52 and produced pictures all his life here.

RW: Subsequently you have become involved in film and photography. Do you chart you interests back to something around those times?

MW: Well in the early days I began to collect things. I rapidly realised that you had to get a specialty and you had to get a focus. So I got into two areas, one was incunabula, books printed before 1500, and I put together a collection of those. I also collected prints and engravings from the French 1850s to the 1900s, and illustrated books from that period, from the United States, England and France. Those were the collections I was most interested in until I started collecting photography around 1978.

RW: Did you start collecting photographs while you were still in the States?

MW: No, I'd moved over here by then. I went back and forth a great deal. I had a friend who I'd gone to university with who was an assistant curator in photography and print at The Metropolitan Museum in New York. I used to go down and go to his house in Soho in New York. It was an interesting time down there and I would meet people like Ralph Gibson and Robert Mapplethorpe, they'd come round for dinner or they'd hang out and talk

about photography. So I was in this milieu and exposed to it, but still hadn't quite made a connection with it.

RW: So were you already interested in photography or was it just this connection with your friend?

MW: I think everyone's interested in photography and I'd always been a person who made photographs and had my own darkroom and did all that. I'd even taught photography as a practical thing to kids. When I was in Washington DC I used to run a classes for ghetto kids in photography. So I had an interest as an amateur maker not as a collector. About 1978 there was a sale at Sotheby's, I'd always gone to auctions, I'd go for auctions of the print stuff. My friend called me up and he said 'I've just looked at the catalogue for a sale and there are twelve things I'd like to purchase for The Metropolitan Museum, would you go and look at them for me.' I said 'I don't know anything about photography as far as evaluating it', he said 'no, you collect works on paper, I just want a condition report.' It had about 350 lots in the sale, I went back and gave him a condition report and he gave me bids to execute. I went along to the sale; all his bids were too low. While I was sitting there I started buying – so he got nothing and I ended up with 60 lots out of the sale. That's when I started collecting.

RW: So it's the Metropolitan Museum that started you buying photography?

MW: Yes. I'm going to give a talk out in California at the end of April about the relationship between the collector and the museum and I think it's interesting how, if you have the right kind of curators and the right kind of atmosphere in the museum, they can stimulate collectors, they can guide collectors; certainly that's been my experience. Then what happens is that as the collector gets more and more experienced he then can become helpful to the museum by becoming a trustee and things like that.

RW: The most obvious thing to come out of that is that you got the work and The Metropolitan couldn't afford to.

MW: Sometimes museum people have that point of view, although the way it is right now they don't have any money to buy anything anyway, no matter what the price was they couldn't really afford it. I said 'forget about them, that's a very short sighted way of looking at it. They're banking all the stuff for you because they aren't going to last for ever. Collectors die, they have estate taxes to pay, eventually everything goes to the museums, the fact that it is delayed for 20 or 30 years is unimportant. If you have a good relationship with the collectors you can borrow it whenever you need it and you know where it is. They're just funding this thing for you and you'll get it later.' It's true that temporarily it's possible the collector is going to have this stuff but we're all just temporary custodians.

RW: Do you feel that your collections, in the past or presently, have had your character in them?

MW: To some extent, the areas in which I collect reflect my character I suppose. I can't make a general statement about what I've tried to collect. I have uses for the collection and I guess I collect with that in mind and that is mostly didactic, educational, for exhibitions and stuff like that.

RW: You said that collections go to national museums, your collection started in America, you're now in Britain, has that become an issue?

MW: You've highlighted a problem that I'd like to correct in England. That is that the English collections, and in France the French collections, are very parochial. One of the reasons I've brought my collection here and am teaching here – mostly art historians, that's who I'm trying to get to – is that this is about the only place you can see really important American work, really important French work, without leaving the country. It's unique in that respect.

RW: Is it important for Britain to maintain its national heritage?

MW: I don't see that it's as important as the British do. That's a kind of political decision to be made. By concentrating on that and spending all their resources on that they end up with very parochial collections, art historians have to go to New York and Paris to see work by other practitioners in the history of photography. Think what the National Gallery would be like if the Impressionists were all English, it would be pretty poor. The fact is that art is an international idea and it moves around at different periods of time. It's the same with photography, by concentrating as they do on the national heritage for photography, they limit themselves terribly. Maybe

RW: You said art but photographs are seen as representing history. Maybe

Roger Fenton's work has as much importance in representing a period of national history as it does in representing the art of photography.

MW: I think those two things are pretty well bound up together and can't be unbound. You pick a good example, the idea that, let's say, Roger Fenton has to be kept in this country is a laudable one but there are enough copies of his work that you don't have to make the decision on every single picture. There are plenty of places that have copies of his work. When was the last time a Roger Fenton show was mounted in England? I can't tell you, maybe about the time he was living. The next Roger Fenton show that is coming to England is being mounted by three museums in the United States; The Metropolitan Museum, The National Gallery and The Getty are pooling their resources and putting together the definitive show of Fenton. So it takes the Americans, to do the definitive show of Fenton and that's because they appreciate it, they have good holdings in their collections, they can put a show together. So you have to ask yourself what's the point in having all the stuff here if that's the reality?

RW: How many of the pictures in your collection are of unknown authorship?

MW: I have a large group of anonymous photographs because I try to collect image rather than necessarily artist. We could count the boxes, I think we'd see maybe forty boxes of early anonymous pictures. Much more than any museum would have by the way because they can't justify acquiring anonymous pictures.

RW: What's your relationship with scholars and art historians?

MW: I was on a panel once where you had a lot of people from the photographic business. I was refered to as 'the end user' in this group. I had to point out that first of all I'm only the temporary holder and conduit, but if anyone's the end user, it's the public, they're the ones that are supposed to go and see those things, to look at them and respond to them. It's the job of the collector to preserve the stuff and the curator to select it and educate the public and give them an insight. There's a scholarly role in this and a critic's role. The critic's role comes at the very end and that's about whether the curator has done a good job, but I think the scholar's job is an interesting one. I think they can enhance the experience of pieces by giving you an insight into them. This can be additional historical knowledge that doesn't appear on the face of the object itself. They also become fairly elaborate in the social criticism and the symbols and the social structure of the day. They can get very far afield from what collectors or the general public are interested in knowing and that tends to be the area where there is some tension with other people.

RW: In comparison to the American market there seems to have been less appreciation of the potential value of photography in Britain.

MW: There's hardly any market here, hardly anyone buys, even today. Almost everything is bought and exported.

RW: Do you have any idea why that is?

MW: I think it's because there are no collectors, and there are no collectors because the government is the big collector, monopolises the whole area. There's no tradition of collecting, there's no tradition of giving either. Americans have a tradition of being involved in museums and local churches, this whole idea of tithing, even if you go beyond religious ideas it's very much engrained in American life so people believe in supporting and giving to hospitals and museums and all kinds of things. It's a different way of operating things. It creates collectors, they buy things museums can't buy, they donate them later.

RW: There were massive collectors of painting and sculpture, why don't you think that has translated to photography?

MW: There are some, but photography is quite recent in collecting. The idea of the wealthy landed gentry collecting is an idea that started to fade even between the wars. But that means that those people who used to do the collecting aren't doing it so who's going to do the collecting? In fact it may be that among some people there is a negative aspect to collecting; you're competing with the government, there's a feeling that somehow it's associated with a time when there was social exploitation; that there may even be a negative aspect to being a collector.

RW: Why didn't you end up collecting contemporary photography as well?

MW: Let's say I like the 19th century, I find it interesting. But there are two issues, one is that you have a limited amount of resources, you have an interest in an area and the area is challenging because you have to exercise connoisseurship. Now, how does that apply to contemporary photography, you're not going to collect anything that's unique, you're only going to collect things that are in big editions and are readily available in other places in museums or private collections. If you want to see a Mapplethorpe you're not going to have any trouble. It takes absolutely no connoisseurship, what are you going to say, that I have number one or number twenty seven, do I get a silver or platinum print? That's as far as you have to go. On the other hand you go to a 19th century piece, and there it is, it's being sold at auction, it's unlikely that anyone has seen it before, is this a good copy or not, what should it look like, if you've seen other copies of this piece is it better or worse than them? You have to

know what you're doing or you make terrible blunders and I've made plenty of them but along the way I've learnt enough so that I can understand what I'm doing. Most of the pictures I have you can't get anywhere else and if you can I try to have the best examples because over the 150 years that they have been around there are very few that are as good as they can be. I want to show people Talbots the way they were supposed to look.

RW: Is there is a diminishing amount of material coming on the market?

MW: Well that's what the dealers tell me. But I keep on getting as much as I can afford because the prices keep going up and I keep on getting good pieces. I'm in a very small market, I would say there are 100 people and maybe 50 or 60 institutions. That's the market, a tiny market but very competitive.

RW: You must know a lot of the other collectors, is there much exchange of information, is it a fraternal grouping or not particularly?

MW: After the last sale we have a party. Everyone who comes to London, the dealers, collectors, who run the auction galleries, everyone comes here and has a drink. It used to be – but people used to go into my office and they'd borrow a knife and cut albums up and divide them up between dealers. So it used to be that wild and wooly but it's got a little more sophisticated. So I meet everyone who's fairly serious in the business, we all socialise, I'm happy to share any information with people and have always felt that people are fairly open with me.

RW: You're giving classes about the work, could you say a little about that?

MW: I've done the course before at the University of California about three years ago. I had seventeen PhD students and three museum curators. I'm doing a similar thing with the Royal College of Art starting this February. We'll cover the history of photography from the beginning to the Second World War in ten weeks. Five of them are practicing photographers on their MA, the rest are art historians working at museums and auction houses.

RW: Could you say what you want people to take away from the experience of seeing these pictures?

MW: I feel that there is a lot of theory and interpretation in art history classes but there is probably less of an appreciation for the aesthetic aspects of photography and looking at a photograph as an object. So I'm just trying to expose people to that idea and by going through the history of photography and looking at good examples people get an understanding of it, so when they get around to curating shows they will be more attuned to this aspect of things as well as the interpretative ones.

HOLDING ON ANDREW ROBINSON

These photographs are from the home of a person with Obsessive Compulsive Disorder (O.C.D.). The contents of the house had been accumulated over the period of a year or more and little if anything had been thrown away during this time.

Narrow walkways led through rooms knee deep in the ephemera of a consumer culture. What might at first appear to be discarded rubbish had to be approached with the care and attention usually reserved for an archeological dig, the movement of items to place camera and lights requiring sensitive negotiation.

Slowly over the course of a number of visits I ventured deeper into the house, initially on the ground floor, then upstairs and into the bathroom. The bedroom however remained out of bounds.

The creation of this collection of artifacts, along with the owners desire to have it recorded before it's enforced clearance, seemed like an attempt to hold on to something past. A desire one can recognise in much photography, the wish to preserve; to capture a fleeting moment.

REVISIONISTS TAKE NOTE

SEAN SEXTON TALKS TO RICHARD WEST. PORTRAIT BY PAUL QUINN.

RW: So tell us then where you were born?

SS: I was born in Co. Clare in 1946 on a small farm, 55 acres, rural, Co. Clare. No running water. My mother never had a pram for any of the seven of us. The farm was worked by hand by my father, it was a dairy farm basically, I think there were eight cows, one horse that was for the ploughing. Turf was cut in the bog by hand, brought home, that was the fuel.

RW: So how much an idea of the family history do you have from when you were growing up?

SS: Very little. When they slated the house, I think in probably 1960, a musket was found underneath the thatch, apparently they were sympathetic to the republican movement. I didn't know that much about the history, our family, especially on the male side. If you think about a stiff upper lip here, you want to see into our house. There was no displays of affection shown to the the children at all from the men, that wasn't a done thing. Then entertainment, we used to go to the local village and it was bloody dreary.

RW: Why did you come to London?

SS: Economics. No jobs, no work, nothing. My first job was stacking the shelves on Anthony Jackson's Food Fair in Iverness Street, Camden Town. That was the first supermarket in the country or one of them anyway. Then I worked in a scrapyard and I worked a stop-and-go sign on the roads. That was tiring, it was awful cold; eventually, I drove a truck for Murphy's. I was already going to the auctions and the markets a bit, and of course I was skiving too I suppose, I can't remember, did I get sacked, or did I pack it in. I think it more likely I got sacked, but I had to go anyway, can't be working for yourself and for Mr. Murphy at the same time. I think I'd got

three thousand quid saved, a fair bit of money and I went to two sales, at Christie's in King Street, and Sotheby's in Belgravia, and I blew the lot.

RW: But that's a long time, that's ten years after you arrived.

SS: Yeah, it's a pity I didn't get in earlier. In the 50s and 60s, stuff was thrown away, literally thrown away. Many, many stories of it, even photographs dumped and burned and frames sold for their value. So anyway in '73 I then started learning and learning was hard. I remember we'd get up at three o'clock or whatever time, and get the night bus down to Blackfriars and then get another night bus from there to go round the antique market. I started going to the auctions, looking in the catalogues, studying left, right and centre, getting to know my subject. And I remember once I was in Brick Lane, it must have been about five o'clock in the morning and there was an English guy there behind one of the stalls and he said 'What's wrong son?', 'Well', I says, 'I can't find the stuff and I haven't got the customers to sell it to.' He says 'right, now I give you a piece of advice, you stick to what you're doing. Its going to be hard in the beginning, and it will take you five to seven years, to start getting there as well.' So that was one piece of advice I got, then the auctions were about to start. I remember there was one in '71, which of course I wasn't there for, there was two in '72 I wasn't there for, both Sotheby's and Christie's and then three a year each from then on when it got into the full swing of things. And and of course the Irish stuff was for nothing, and I thought, well I'll collect that, I know enough about it, and I know a bit about the history. It's very easy to fall by the wayside you know. Another collector as well was Howard Rickets, he was quintessentially English, went to Winchester and all that, said 'Sean Sexton, you keep collecting your Irish photographs'.

RW: Was there anyone else that you met, who was doing the same thing?

SS: There weren't many, there weren't many dealers, there never have been in London, because basically the attitude in England or anywhere in Britain to photography was that they just take photos, they never regard it as an art – they still don't. Whereas the French and the Americans are different, and other people as well.

RW: So why did you buy cameras? Did you ever think you would use them?

SS: No, I wanted to collect them, and then of course I knew after a while that I just couldn't go on with it, because I'd spend all my money in a couple of sales, and then I had to start buying and selling, and then I really got some rare cameras. Later on, I mean this is 1979, I had a Hunter & Sands which later became Sands & Hunter gun camera, and there were only two in the world, one in the Science Museum, and one which I had, that I paid five thousand for, and that was a lot of money then. There was nothing to guide me, it was so rare, it had never appeared at auction, you couldn't look it up. Now here's the wheeling and dealing which I am fairly good at I think. I picked up the phone and phoned Spira, he's a big collector of cameras, head of the Spiratone Corporation in America. So I offer him the camera. I phoned Leeve Price in Norway, had one of the biggest museums in Horton in Norway, and I offered him the camera at twenty thousand, so he kind of hmmd and hawed, he had plenty of money and wanted to come to some kind of arrangement. I was never very good at the mathematics and I said thanks, bye. I was afraid certain collectors

might get in cahoots and decide that they wouldn't take the price over a certain amount. Down with the phone, up with the phone, over to New York, phoned Spira in New York. I then offered him the camera at fifteen thousand, but I wasn't going to drop below that, I knew how rare it was. So he was so sure of himself, I think he offered me ten, and said take my time, come back to him in a couple of weeks, and he gave me basically a spiel about times, prices weren't high and all this stuff. Up with the phone again and back to Norway and I said Leeve, I'll make you an offer you just can't refuse, it's fifteen thousand, five thousand pounds down now, and ten thousand to be paid next May. He says 'You've got a deal. Done.' He hadn't even seen the camera.

RW: You took this picture at the time.

SS: Yes. And I put a ruler on them so you get an idea. An absolutely fabulous piece, and I had to explain very carefully at London airport, and say, 'look what I've got in here, I don't want to get shot, I have here, a camera in the shape of a machine gun.' They were bloody fascinated. They'd seen some things but they'd never seen anything like that. So anyway. I went to Norway, and I got picked up at the airport and that. He spent a whole day showing me around the museum. I do believe he gave it to the Norwegian nation afterwards.

RW: So when you first started, this is the early seventies, where would be your happiest hunting ground for looking for photographs?

SS: Portabello Road has always been very good to me, I like the place very much. It wasn't as early in the morning. I remember at seven, eight o'clock, somehow at the time when the sun is about to rise, I think the cold rushes up the Thames and really gets into your bones. There's all this thing on television, The Antiques Roadshow and that, they never see the hard side of things, as dealers would have it, driving down from Scotland or from Cornwall the night before, and they go out and kill themselves, they die young, on the odd occasion falling asleep behind the wheels of their cars. Very unsociable occupation, all the marriages I know and liasons, have broken up. I know only one marriage that held. You come in then from Portabello, back at four o'clock in the afternoon, you're knackered, you go to bed, your wife wants you to go out shopping.

RW: Why do people do it?

SS: They do it for the love. Some do it for the money but the people who do it for money usually fall by the wayside, because they won't stick to it. There's very little money to be made.

RW: Going back a bit, you started to meet other collectors.

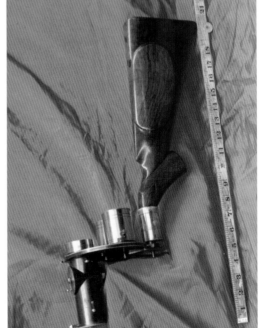

Courtesy of Sean Sexton

another Irish collector who collects postcards, actually a friend of mine, you should never mix friendship and collecting, business. He approached me once and said he wanted to take half the market, and I'd take the other half so we didn't bid against one another. I said to him 'I'll tell you what you can do, I'll stay in my place and you stay in your place if we don't we'll start bidding against one another and money'll start going out of our pockets into other people's pockets and we'll both be very sorry. But I will invade your territory if you invade mine. End of story'.

RW: But when there is only one other person doing it, then it really is your territory.

SS: It doesn't work like that, about four years ago now, there was an album came up of the British military in Ireland and elsewhere, extensive album something like 200 photographs. There were photographs of Irish workers, I hesitate to use the word peasants. Three of them are beaters, they'd beat the gorse so they could shoot the pheasants. Of course those were the images I wanted. It's 1850s, 1857, the estimate on this album was £1,500 or thereabouts. I knew the British army collectors would be after all the British army stuff. Also in there were three photographs of Victoria Cross winners and also in there was a photograph of the liason guy between the British government and the American confederacy in the American civil war, so there was obviously important stuff in there. Anyway the bidding started and the British army collectors put up the white flag at £7,000. Then I had to take on the Victoria Cross guys, one of whom finances, I believe, the Conservative Party. He surrendered at £30,000, it was £25,000 pus the 10% or whatever it was. That's what you call auction fever, you can just get carried away, especially if you've got a mesmeric auctioneer. Auctioneers can really flatter your ego, you have to be careful, they're going 'you're not going to let him get away with that are you' and it'll go up up up. It only takes two people.

RW: Did you get to know all the people who are interested in collecting Irish photography?

SS: There never were that many people, there's Eddie Chandler in Dublin, but we have two different approaches. The best thing is to bring it out into the open. I bring out all aspects of Irish life, I have done it in books and exhibitions. What is remarkable in his history is the lack of controversial material; 1916, evictions etc. and what have you. I have to go off in a different direction to the revisionists. During all this time I was noting the revisionists including the wonderful professor Foster and all the rest of them, whitewashing, watering down, rewriting Irish history. It's Irish historians mostly, not British historians, I have no complaint with them. They couldn't be seen to be writing about the Fenians, evictions, 1916, the

Republican movement. That's what it's all down to one way or another. If you were going to use the yardstick of the Second World War when you were writing about the Napoleonic wars then you're not a bloody historian, that's OK as a stage play or something. There I am coming across eviction photographs – there are several books here, there's Foster's one and a couple of others – under these photographs it says 'possibly staged photographs' or 'these manipulated photographs', etc. Muddying the waters, whitewashing, etc. Let me say now on the record: who do they think they are? At the time of the evictions, especially the County Clare ones which are well recorded, the British army was present which kept records. The RIC kept records, and kept accurate records as well. Sometimes there were magistrates who were actually at the scene who kept records. There were correspondents from the *Times* there, local papers and some international correspondants who kept records, there were four or five different ones. That's first rate history. To turn around and rubbish that. Photography has found out the revisionists. Here's another important point, before the Boer war photography was hardly ever manipulated or doctored, there's only a couple of exceptions, one was with the Communards, or to do with that in the 1870s in Paris when I think they superimposed heads on bodies and stuff like this. The rot started when technically they started to reproduce photographs in newspapers, I think there was a German newspaper in 1904 but I think particularly *The Mirror* in 1905.

RW: How does this express itself when you're in the sale room or actually collecting the photographs?

SS: I collect everything there is. Having said that, my Irish collection is weak in certain areas. It's got great strengths, there's no doubt about that, it's recognised as that, and there are some now who say that it's better than the national collection in Dublin. I don't know what the national collection would comprise of, if you're talking about cini footage then they win it hands down because they have stuff on 1916, some very great stuff indeed, very fine stuff. But as far as still stuff is concerned before 1900 I think I have it because a lot of my stuff is hand picked. There is a lot of stuff in the Lawrence collection that is very boring indeed. They've done a fine job in rounding up that collection for £300 in 1941 I think it was.

RW:. In the sale room is there anyone else who's been collecting this stuff, that you've been trying to get hold of?

SS: There are, I went to a sale in Dublin, there was one guy who put a whole collection together, it's about two years ago, the stuff was lotted by county, it was street scenes mostly, and all the historical societies came from the counties – not to say a raider, a thief from London – I had the

Black and Tans, lest they could be seen as being sympathetic to the present money of course, my rival was there, he wanted to do a deal, I said forget it. I was just determined, I just made it so fucking hot that no one could come near me. I got near the whole sale, there were nearly 30 lots in it.

RW: It's interesting you're saying this, talking about Foster's book and collecting all this stuff, you're saying that the photographs you've collected are an historical account in themselves.

SS: They are, and they can't ignore them, it gives the lie to some of the awful lot of English people. My collection has been put together with the help of an awful lot of English people. There are gaps which I would like to fill, one is traditional Irish musicians, Irish Gaelic games I haven't got much of. That's where Dublin scores, they have a lot of that stuff, good luck to them. You can see that I've got to that stage where I can bid and not care too much about the money. Because of the Charles Jones archive, and that was in Bermondsey antique market in 1981 at 9 o'clock in the morning. It had been going since 3 o'clock in the morning. I was there late and came across a trunk load of photographs that everyone had turned down. The guy had put them away under the stall, the guy didn't even want to show them to me. I looked, I took out a group of photographs of turnips, carrots, parsnips and I was astounded. Even though I judge everything historically my eye is artistically orientated, always has been, for photography in general. I bought the whole collection for X amount, I've been selling them ever since. I only put three or four through the auction houses every year. They used to sell for £2-300 then they took a jump one year and now they fetch £6-700. Eventually I brought out a book and the price has just gone up and up. They now sell through Davis Langdale gallery in New York for up to £8,000 each, and they are selling.

RW: You said you get the impression that Irish organisations or museums were seeing that you were collecting stuff and were bidding against you?

SS: I know that the National Library of Ireland has bid against me several times but they will very seldom tell you what their agenda is, and vice versa. I can outbid them anyway. But Gráinne MacLochlainn came over two years ago and there were two albums of photographs taken at Rockingham, landed gentry basically. There were two lots, one very decorative album which they now have, the second lot was two albums, the sister to the first lot. So I arrived at Christie's in South Ken and somebody said 'there's a woman looking for you, she's up there.' 'Excuse me, I believe you've been looking for me', Gráinne MacLochlainn, never met her before, I said 'I think I know why you're here, would you ever do me a favour and get a taxi back out to London airport and go back to Ireland.' She said 'look Sean, if you let us have the two lots', 'you can't have them'. She said 'look Sean, if you let us have the two lots we'll let you have copies for your collection. 'I don't have copies,

originals only.' I says 'you're going to have your work cut out here today, there's only one way out of it, you take one lot and I'll take the other.' She agreed which was the sensible thing to do, keep it, as it were, within the family. Because I said to her 'you'll have no problem here from the English collectors or the Irish collectors, your problem is going to be from the American collectors', which proved to be true. That was a case of keep it sensible, don't let it away to other people.

RW: Talking about the telling of history and the National Library trying to collect stuff, should these pictures go to a certain home?

SS: I'll tell you now, if I can find it that is... Right Santiago Calatrava, an architect I greatly admire, maybe he's a bit too symplistic though, there are other architects. Imagine something like that in the West of Ireland not in Dublin – they've got enough already – to house the collection.

RW: How are you going to organise this?

SS: It might have been better to try and organise something like this two or three years ago and go to the relevant minister because with the Irish economy the way it is, they might not be that amenable to listen to you. Or why not have it here in London? That's another part of my experience of London, and I'm 40 years in it now, there are no cultural outlets for the Irish, nothing. No big museums, no collections, bits and bobs here in the British Library and all the rest of it. Damn all.

RW: What plans do you have for the collection?

SS: I've just told you, but that's just an idea at the end of the day, you've got to be practical. I certainly wouldn't want it to end up in the Irish archive in Dublin which is an unsuitable place buried away. The problem is that with Ireland's literary reputation with Yeats, Joyce, whom I'm a great admirer of by the way, they see the archive as an adjunct to the library but it's not. Photography has a voice in its own right, it's not there to illustrate literature, it's a challenge.

RW: What about other institutions?

SS: It needs a gallery of photography. The archive just for the sake of a little bit of space could have been good. You need a proper museum for photography, but what are the chances for that now? There is a good way around that of course, trundle on over, Galway's a good spot, or Clare. Have you seen the folklore place at Castlebar? They must have spent 7 or 8 million on it. There is a case for a thing like that à la Calatrava. There's an Iranian architect Zaha Hadid who's very good. So there you are. They say what the hell's it doing in storage in Enfield, it should be seen. If someone had to put that collection together it couldn't be done. Even if you got a

RW: You are in a position with this collection, to tell a different story.

SS: You can contextualise it as much as you like and use as many academic words as you like. This is where photography differs from the written word. You can be a very clever academic and juggle all the words and throw them up in the air and come out with what you want to prove. There are statistics there to prove it anyway. I teamed up with Christine Kineally. I approached her after I read her book on the famine, *The Great Calamity*. What we decided about this book was that we were going to keep it low key, no emotive language, no superlatives and keep as factual as we could. I chose all the photographs in the book and Thames and Hudson gave me total freedom. Totally English company, there's about 120 work in that office, never once did they say lean it the nationalist way, lean it the British way, never once.

RW: Of your total collection how many of the photographs have been published in the books?

SS: 460, there's 20,000 photographs altogether. But don't forget, and here's where revisionism ought to take note, I've done a deal with Bill Gates' company Corbis. They're a picture agency, they get stuff published in magazines and newspapers all over the world. That was about 6 years ago.

RW: How did that all come about, what are they like to work with?

SS: They're very good but one thing I insist on with picture agencies, very hard to enforce though, I said to them whatever is published I don't want it digitised, enhanced, cropped, falsified in any way. The photographs must be reproduced as the photographer took them. Or, it's like in the *Guardian* magazine here, they asked me if I would agree to cropping one of the most important photographs in the book and that's the eviction photograph. They've cropped it and in retrospect I would not now have agreed with it but they said they would put 'detail'. So that's OK, you're not misleading anybody. It has ruined the photograph but then it says 'detail' so go and look up the full picture. I think this is very important, as far as I'm concerned this is evidence at the court of human history.

RW: Have Corbis scanned everything in your collection?

SS: They've scanned a lot of it but I've kept some stuff back in case I need to do another publication. The contract with them, which goes for 20 years, I regret now because they scanned some Charles Jones images which are now out of my control. Charles Jones material I'm very strict with, never thrown around the place, never much released. It's being shown in public

institutions like the Modern Museum of Art in San Francisco, the Botanical Gardens in Chicago, the most prestigious of the lot is in Gottenburg, and that was the Hasselblad exhibition about 2 years ago, and that was very prestigious. They give an annual award and one particular year they didn't give an award because the standard wasn't good enough. Usually when they have an award of the winner they have a vintage exhibition to counterpoint it and that was Charles Jones. It was wonderful walking up to the museum because there were two big banners down the front of the building and one said 'the work of Paul Gaugin' and the other said 'the photographs of Charles Jones.' Then there's the private galleries, Davis Langdale in New York which is a very important gallery in that it introduced Lucien Freud to America. This catalogue for instance they have various artists including a drawing by Matisse and the only photograph in it is a Charles Jones photograph. Even with private galleries it has to be a first rate gallery, it has to be top flight. This is where I get back to Corbis and I have to have a meeting with them, they were licensing out stuff and it was being used in places I wouldn't be seen dead. What I'm trying to pursuade them is that it's gilt edged, first rate, you charge a lot or nothing. That's how I protect that.

RW: How does that work, that's just on availability then. You don't own the copyright to the pictures?

SS: No you don't that's a misnomer, I own permission to reproduce because I own the originals. The copyright has run out.

RW: This means that for a fee Corbis gives access to the pictures in your collection?

SS: They get access and they even get a thumbnail sketch and if you want the thing then you have to give your credit card or whatever. But when they copied the photographs they copied them with a scanner, this is eight years ago, I've been saying to them the quality's not high enough. I operate with an art group in town and they said that the quality of the scans from Corbis was just not high enough.

RW: So there are a lot of photographs that haven't been published?

SS: Yes but the important ones are there. I could certainly do another book. I could see myself doing one on evictions, from a very scientific, clinical level, statistics, etc, just to nail the revisionists' lie.

A NEW BLUE CARPET
STEPHEN MCCOY

A new blue carpet and a new Dyson vacuum cleaner. The clear cylinder filling with a cyclone of carpet fibres. Settling down. Shelves – drilling into brick and vacuuming afterwards, red dust over the top of blue turning to grey. Car cleaning – small stones and gravel. Christmas aftermath – pine needles, tinsel. Fingernail parings, hair and more food crumbs. All layering down and providing an archaeological document of houshold activities.

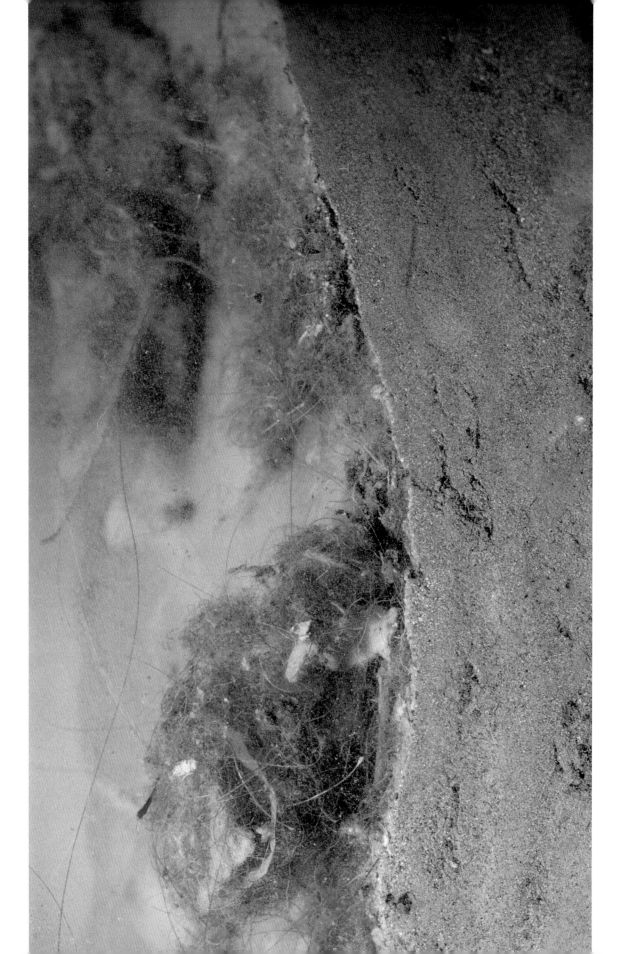

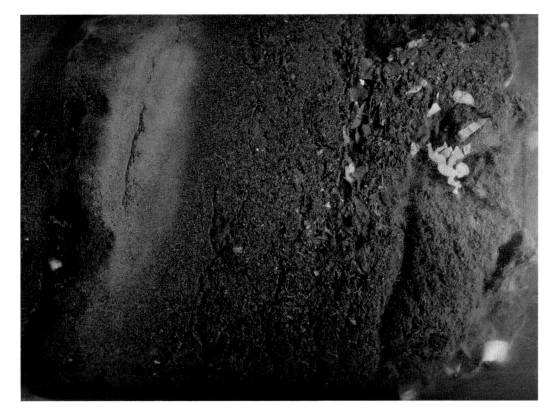

EXHIBITION REVIEWS

PSYCHO-GEOGRAPHY
HIRSCHL FINE ART

JOEL STERNFIELD
PHOTOGRAPHER'S GALLERY

DAVID GOLDBLATT
MOMA OXFORD

MARIO GIACOMELLI
PHOTOFUSION

PETER BOBBY
MISSION GALLERY

SHARON YA'ARI
LISSON GALLERY

engaging landscapes

Psycho-geography photographs by Sian Bonnell, Paul Cunningham and Jem Southam. Hirschl Contemporary Art, 5 February - 8 March

The idea of an artistic engagement with landscape is irrevocably associated with the Romantic movement and this is a burden that contemporary artists referencing landscape have to bear, or at least have to bear in mind. All three photographers in this show engage with this dilemma, each in their own way, whether that be Jem Southam's exploration of the temporal shifts in mood that can totally transform the demeanour of a landscape, Paul Cunningham's highlighting of the idiosyncrasies visited upon the landscape by man's activities there, or Sian Bonnell's reduction of landscape to a contextual backdrop, against which she arrays a series of constructed scenes.

Despite the humorous veneer of Sian Bonnell's constructed landscape images, the apparent whimsicality of these images conceals a serious critical engagement with issues of feminism and environmental abuse. There is a tussle in these unorthodox images between the forces of levity and gravity, the ascendancy of either dependant upon the way in which the viewer perceives them. From an Aesthetic point view, the series of C-prints in this show, titled Putting Hills in Holland, fall somewhere between the baroque and the surreal. In the foreground of these photographs are somewhat sculptural constructions built up using collections of domestic objects such as jelly-moulds, cakes and cut flowers, set against backdrops of the Dutch landscape, telling us very little about Holland, but hinting instead at the tradition of Dutch still-life painting. The symmetry of these constructions, however, brings them right up to date, giving them the appearance of zany, rather benign robots. The most engaging image of this series, *Putting Hills in Holland I*, is also the simplest, a china cup decorated with a stylised mountainous landscape, provides not only the in-focus punctum, but also the topographical drama in a landscape of otherwise unrelievedly bleak flatness – we feel deprived of little by the out-of-focus blur which holds this scene back from our gaze. The irony here is that this cup, a notionally romantic creation designed to bring the sentimentalised beauty of an idealised landscape into our homes, rescues us here from the monotony of a real landscape.

Jem Southam's quiet series of seven images, titled *River Culm at Rewe*, have a tranquil meditative feel about them. Becoming absorbed in these images – taken between 1995 and 2003 – is akin to listening to the grass grow. The grass not only grows here, but is frequently inundated, and you don't need to be a trained geographer to appreciate the dramatic changes that sweep across this landscape during the duration of this series. All taken from the same view point, but at different times of the day and through different seasons – in the same vein as his earlier series on the Devon Coast or the Isle of Wight – these photographs simply do not look like images of the same scene, until you look closer and begin to recognise the repeated configurations of the treescape in the middle distance. Images of the river in spate, or in flood, the flood subsiding, or the meadows blanketed in snow, all convey totally different scenes. While Paul Cezanne used variations in painting technique to transform that vista towards Mont Sainte Victoire, in France, Southam, somewhat closer to Monet and his Haystacks series, simply lets nature and time do the work. Not only do we register these landscape transformations snatched from the flow of time, but we try to imagine the evolution of which these images are but a fragment – to quote Jacques Lacan, 'That from which time makes a stuff is not borrowed from the imaginary, but rather from a textile where the knots speak of nothing but the holes that are there'.

Photographers have always sought out the unique, the novel and the downright bizarre things of this world upon which to feed their lenses. Often they fail because the results look too studied, too precious or too trite. Paul Cunningham, in his travels around England, shows an uncanny gift for pinpointing the sense of place, and particularly the foibles of that place. He is able to succinctly summarise a location through the lens of his camera, this is not something that can be learned, it is purely intuitive. If it were to be learned it would become formulaic. Cunningham's images are almost invariably fresh, and often oblique in concept. In his image, *Untitled 5*, a forest of brightly coloured cranes, cherry-pickers and hydraulic platforms reach for the sky from a wacky collection of scissored, telescopic and articulated arms, seemingly engaged in some sort of cybernetic feeding frenzy. Amputated as they are by the bases by the viewing angle of the camera, the context remains a mystery and the spectacle becomes sublimely surreal. His *Untitled 38*, could not be more of a contrast, here a forest of dead and dry stems of invasive weeds punctuates the paving of a traffic island, whose refuge has obviously long been shunned – a no-mans land that is in the first throes of a return to nature. Cunningham's apparent sympathy in raising this scene from its ignominy, carries a wry irony that is as sharp as a razor.

Diametrically opposed in their approach to landscape, these three photographers would not, one would think, make likely companions, however,

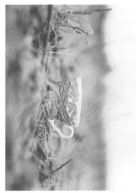

Opposite: *Untitled 5*, Paul Cunningham

Top left: *Putting the Hills in Holland 1*,
Sian Bonnell
Top right: *Putting the Hills in Holland 12*,
Sian Bonnell

Above: *The River Culm at Rewe, 5*
Jem Southam

the resonance set up by the contrasts of their images makes for fascinating viewing. The intentionality of each of these photographers is thrown into sharp relief by the presence of the others, turning an exhibition which might have proved a risky experiment, into a successful venture.

Roy Exley

american nature

Joel Sternfeld was at the Photographer's Gallery, London
29 November - 18 January 2003

Joel Sternfeld is a well established and influential figure in contemporary American photography, but he has not been widely shown in the UK and Europe. His recent exhibition at the Photographer's Gallery, *Joel Sternfeld*, is his first solo show in England and offered a long awaited introduction to his work. Would that it had been more comprehensive. It focuses primarily on a recently published body of portraits, *Strangers Passing*, and throws in for a bit of background a handful of images from his seminal series *American Prospects*, made in the late 70s and early 80s. While I can see the necessity of including the *American Prospects* work – it shares many of the same interests with just a slight shift in emphasis – stuck away in the back room of the gallery it seems an afterthought, incidental rather than integral. A much stronger show could have been carved out of these two bodies of work by allowing a dialogue between the earlier and later images.

America and Americans are at the center of this work. In the ongoing photographic and literary tradition of examining what constitutes America as a nation and culture, Sternfeld's work adds an important chapter. Much of his oeuvre is an investigation into the intersection of American nature and its culture. He teases out the essences and contradictions between a land and its people. *American Prospects* best realises this. It has a wonderful strangeness that hovers in the banality of much of its subject matter. The simulacra waves in the pool of the *Wet and Wild Aquatic Theme Park* seem to hint at something untoward lurking beneath the friendly veneer of this entertainment venue in Orlando, Florida; the perfect match of colour between the ice plant growing on an L.A. hillside in *Rustic Canyon, Santa Monica, California, May 1979*, and the car parked beside it, speaks of an uncanny congruence between that natural and man-made American world. It is this curious tension in the imagery – as if all the parts don't quite match up – that makes *American Prospects* so remarkable. Sternfeld doesn't quite explain America in these photographs; They aren't emblematic pictures. In fact, the more opaque and mysterious America becomes in this work, the better we

Opposite: *McLean, Virginia, December 1978*
Courtesy Pace/MacGill Gallery, New York

seem to understand it.

Sternfeld began making portraits during the work of *American Prospects* and these form an important component of that series. *Strangers Passing* seems a continuation of that work, with many of the earliest portraits dating from the mid – late 80s as *Prospects* was ending. But though these images remain environmental portraits, each one particularly defined by locale, the landscape is clearly a secondary concern. Sternfeld uses it more to argue for topographical relativity in the typologies he draws in *Strangers Passing*, than to offer it as an entity unto itself. It is this that clearly separates it from *American Prospects*. The focus here is on the cultural character of the person pictured, and in this respect, Sternfeld is inevitably indebted to August Sander. Sternfeld uses these portraits to detail how the geography of place imprints itself upon the people and persona of a country. *Man Standing on the Banks of the Mississippi, Baton Rouge, Lousiana, August, 1985* perhaps captures this best. A man in overalls, ruggedly hewn, stands on the banks of the mighty Mississippi, as it is so necessarily invoked. He is what we think about when we think about the Mississippi River – at least if you are American – and when we think about him, we are likely to picture the brown expanse of river somewhere nearby. Tallying up the markers of identity, I read him as a bible thumping Baptist, ready to bless you and birth you anew. Whether this is what he really is, I do not know. But he fits in the picture. And so does the lawyer with his laundry in New York, and the woman in her exercise gear in Malibu, or the kids in the intersection of an empty suburban street.

Though I am an enthusiastic fan of Sternfeld's work, I had a gnawing disappointment in the *Strangers Passing* work. Something of the complexity and richness of Sternfeld's vision had been drained in favour of simple associations. I couldn't quite believe that the marks of place are so inevitably embedded in the unique character of individuals – it seemed a kind of 'location' profiling where instead of racial characteristics it is the qualities of locale that mark you. Such generalities can be appealing, satisfying your expectations in a way that makes you feel more comfortable in the world. But they are, unfortunately, rather less interesting than the exceptions, contradictions and anomoloies.

Alicia Miller

small signs of affection

Fifty-one years by David Goldblatt was at The Museum of Modern Art, Oxford. 1 February - 30 March 2003

David Goldblatt's documentary photography in South Africa is distinct from so much of the photojournalism that has come out of its violent history of oppression. Having said how he 'felt no driving need to record those situations and moments of extremity that were the stuff of the media', he was instead drawn to 'the quiet and commonplace where nothing happened and yet all was contained and immanent.' Some of the photography on show in this major retrospective, spanning a period of over half a century, looks back to the American documentary tradition of the 1930s: echoes of the classical formality of Walker Evans's pictures, a sensitivity to the posture and gesture of the body which recalls Dorothea Lange's portraiture.

The current show groups and organises his photographs into what Goldblatt refers to as 'essays,' many of them edited sequences from his books. His earliest and most activist photographs from the '50s, share the first room with his essay, *Particulars*, from the 1970s, a series which as well as demonstrating his more oblique and indirect response to the political upheavals of his country, introduces the emphasis on physicality which runs through much of his photography: sensual close-up details of people – showing hands held in laps, crossed legs – inviting us to read the physical effects of apartheid through gesture, posture and clothing.

The phenomenological accent in his photography – Goldblatt has said how he wanted to explore 'the grit and taste and touch of things' – is of especial importance in his series *Some Afrikaners Photographed*. As a Jewish white male, born of immigrant parents, Goldblatt was brought up in a middle-class family in a suburb of Johannesburg on the Witwatersrand, the gold-bearing reef of South Africa. His pictures of Afrikaners, responding to the kind of people he grew up with as a child, his fear at their racism and physical confidence, are nevertheless edged with ambivalence. While some evidence confrontational aggression and power – white nationalists staring to camera from horseback – others are more sensitive and tender: the symbolically transgressive touch between a white farmer boy and his black nursemaid whose hand playfully holds the heel of his bare foot. Such signs of human affection and tenderness resist and challenge the ideology and law of apartheid. But at the same time inevitably point to a future when this child as an adult will have to deny such intimacy and affection. Another early essay documents the declining mining industries of his hometown: the most visceral and expressive pictures, and certainly the most spectacular, highlight the

dangerous work of the shaftsinkers, who drill and blast and dig mines, working up to fourteen hours a day. But in evidencing the physical hardships of labour, his later series *The Transported of KwaNdebele* is just as powerful. As in the mine photographs, chiaroscuro lighting effects simplify and give graphic force and presence to the pictures. Goldblatt travelled with black South Africans, both men and women, on the crowded buses to and from the homelands and their places of employment, some journeying up to eight hours per day to get to and from work. The images draw out a general condition of subjugation: visibly evident in the gestures and expression of the exhausted workers, as they try to catch what little sleep they can.

The pictures Goldblatt took when he entered the Soweto black township are remarkable for their empathy, despite his own position as outsider to the communities he was picturing. Many of the photographs testify to the trust and respect built up between the photographer and his subjects: epitomised by the portrait showing the gracefulness and sensuality of the singer, Margaret Mcingana, eyes closed, relaxed and reclining in her home. Only the scratches on the back brick wall begin to hint at the violence and struggle all around. In contrast, his series *In Boksburg* offers an acerbic observation of the social mores of a middle class suburbia, similar to the place he grew up in. These pictures testify to a more distanced and anthropological gaze than those in the township; one senses his anger here. Many of those pictured are not engaged with Goldblatt, but are observed going about their daily life. But this catalogue of public and private events is not without a certain ambivalence and contradiction. There is an underlying empathy and fascination with the figure of the child and younger people in this culture: the apprehensive little boy boxer standing rigid in the corner of the ring before a fight; the somewhat awkward display of young girls in the *Miss Lovely Legs Competition*, an exclusive all-white competition which as a result presents us with an unusual exchange of display and gaze between the black people in the audience and those on stage. Or the striking picture of a young teenage girl in her new tutu proudly pirouetting on point. Goldblatt pictures her appearing to be caught in the web of shadows from the trellis on her veranda, just as she is entrapped, we are lead to infer, by the ideology she is being brought up in.

The largest essay in the show documents the structures of South Africa, part of his recent book, *The Structure of Things Then*. During the most violent period of apartheid in the 1980s, Goldblatt began travelling around the country in a camper van photographing its architecture. The series sets up a dialectic between the monstrosity of public monuments, emblematic of Afrikaner Nationalism, and temporary provisional structures like his picture of a coffee cart, a bricolage structure salvaged from material from the white suburbs, or the ruinous evidence of broken homes and businesses following the forced resettlement of non-white communities. Special fascination in the

series is given to the Reformed Church architecture and how it reflects the political changes in his country. The churches built between the '40s and '60s aggressively dominated the landscape, their megaphonic structures broadcasting the word of God and Nationalism out to the country. But as the apartheid state weakened in the '70s and '80s, so churches built in this time tended to have fewer openings piercing their outer walls, they became closed inward looking structures, preaching was done to those within not without. The colour photography, digitally desaturated, which brings the show to a chronological close, continues the dialectic which characterises his *Structures* series, highlighting the visible differences the new economic prosperity has brought to his homeland. Only there is a certain optimism now in his portraits of the emergent class of labourers and traders who are beginning to establish a place and status in the new post-apartheid South Africa. Goldblatt presents these portraits alongside pictures of their subjects' striking homemade signs, advertising their skills, which proliferate Johannesburg city. On the other hand there is a greater sense of derision and contempt, particularly evident in his series of pictures, presented as mock adverts, of real estate development in Northern Johannesburg, a fortified English oasis, only disrupted by the sewer pipe – ludicrously disguised as an aqueduct – which runs right through it, a splendid levelling symbol.

Mark Durden

Opposite: *Erickson the Tiler at Work, Linden, Johannesburg, 1 Jan 2000*

Above left: *Dutch Reformed Church, Quellerina, Johannesburg, November, 1986*

Above right: *Going to Work on the bus, 1984*

the price for life

Mario Giacomelli was at Photofusion, London, 15 November - 1 February

'Photography is not difficult', according to Mario Giacomelli, 'as long as you have something to say'. His declaration inverted a defence of photography commonly deployed in the now largely won battle to grant it artistic status, in which its difficulty is asserted against claims that it is only a matter of pointing a camera, pressing a button and documenting an event. Yet Giacomelli's technical off-handedness was neither a dismissal of photography's sophistication nor of its status as art. His photography testifies as much by showing that he had plenty to say and that he could say it eloquently. The literal and figural, tonal and emotional range of his photographs is broad. There is a striking variation of styles employed in them. They are composed, taken and processed with great care. Despite this Giacomelli was no more an aesthete than he was a documentarist. He was sometimes happy to confront viewers of his work with ugly, disturbing subject-matter and was relatively untroubled by the enraged reactions this elicited. In any case the overall quality of his work is undeniable, whether attributions of pictorialism or brutalism to it are justifiable or not.

Mario Giacomelli was born, lived and died in the Eastern Coastal Italian village of Senegallia during the last three quarters of the twentieth century. He began taking photographs when he was twenty-eight. The subjects depicted in them, with greater and lesser degrees of abstraction, mostly comprised the people, objects and landscapes of the area within a ten-mile radius of his home. These were usually rural, traditional and impoverished. Representations of farm workers, gypsies and priests were produced alongside depictions of the disabled, the mentally ill and the old and dying. Ancient villages, coastal regions and working farms were reproduced too, as were the organic edifices, barren shorelines and scarred fields that marked them out. Giacomelli's is a photography of both hard and soft discriminations. Black-robed figures – priests, mourners – are caught fallen into spare, irregular patterns, the graphicity of which is accentuated over brilliant white grounds. Ugly and gorgeous peasants of all ages are shot in clear but shallow focus alongside their blurred compatriots.

This description of Giacomelli's photography makes it sound provincial and realistic. In some senses (and only in some senses) it is. In a text written for the exhibition and in an essay accompanying a recent collection of Giacomelli's work, Alistair Crawford usefully traces the indirect or unacknowledged influence of early and mid-century realist photography on it. The postwar period in Italy saw the increasing use of documentary photography in popular magazines, particularly those under the picture-editorship of Luigi Crocenzi. Tendentially left-wing, it exposed the poverty, hardship and privation endured by many Italian citizens during the period of Fascism and the war. This confrontational documentarism and the photo-essay form that it was often presented in had been pioneered abroad by 1940's American magazines like *Life* whose ethos was instructed by now well-known Farm Security Administration photographers of the 1930's such as Dorothea Lange and Walker Evans. Their influential contemporary Paul Strand had even shot and published such work in Italy. By the end of the war all of the aforementioned 'straight' but political international and national forms were active in Italian culture. Their effect coincided with and was compounded by Italian neorealist cinema which employed similar cinematographic and ideological tactics.

Giacomelli's work shows clear signs of having been marked by all of these historical and cultural forces. His depictions of disabled and disturbed people are unflinching yet humane and employ a finely-judged combination of verisimilar and aesthetic qualities. Asymmetrical grids or long elegant curved lines of wheelchairs are shot from aside and above at Lourdes. The muscular and psychological obliquity of the faces of the mentally ill is moderate and shot at medium range. It's discretion means that we presume these people are like us before we wonder whether they're not. Pathos, melodrama and sentimentality are avoided in these pictures at all costs.

Yet there was one thing that Giacomelli thought was too dear to pay for that he felt bound to protest about: life, or rather the dreadful end that death brings to it. His photographs of old and dying people compel us to witness the indignity of their panic, isolation, and physical and mental decomposition. These anti-portraits disgust us, and are meant to since they convey what Giacomelli described as his 'revulsion for the price which is paid for life'. There is a particularly modern anguish in these pictures caught between a Catholic 'hope' that 'there's a life after death' and a grave postwar secular Sartrean doubt about this, manifest in an anxious effort to face reality and mortality. Giacomelli snapped a young, chic, alien 'Existentialist' at the same time that he portrayed a dying old woman her arms raised in useless or profound supplication.

The artistry of these photographs reminds us that despite having

Martin Murray

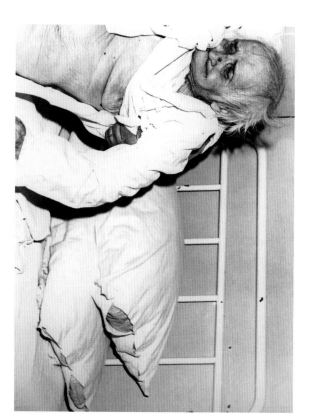

Opposite: Anna, from *Early Work, 1953-1956*

Above: from the series *Lullaby 1985-1987* created from pictures taken 1955-1987

been influenced by realist photography, Giacomelli cannot rightly be classed as a documentarist. He was a painter before he took up the camera and his pictures clearly evoke modern painterly avant-gardes. Surrealist tropes are manifold. The bleached bare architecture of Scanno is haunted by figures swathed in black who seem as inhuman as the statuary that haunt the melancholy townscapes of Giacomelli's compatriot de Chirico (both artists' work anticipate the austere, real and unreal cityscapes shot later by Fellini and Antonioni). The face of the woman in the seated portrait accompanying this review has been blanked like the veiled face of Magritte's dead mother in his painting of a dream about her. The motive tangle of branches above her is expressionistic. Some of Giacomelli's shots of black trees and twisted iron against gray skies as well as of mottled, blanched, rotting walls even amount to a kind of abstract expressionism. His renowned overexposed aerial landscapes of curving, furrowed fields are like colour field paintings without the colour and, since Giacomelli sometimes directed the ploughing of the fields himself, count as an early example of land art. He said that like so much of his art, they were meant to evoke death, in this case of the land. He died himself two years ago. His photographs will have a much longer and better-known life than he did, which is the least his own life and art deserves.

hot from corporate land

Reception by Peter Bobby was at Mission Gallery, Swansea, 7 February - 29 March

A torrid heat seems to emanate from *Reception I (2000)*, Peter Bobby's large-scale photograph of a daringly-designed and recently-completed reception area somewhere in corporate land. The back-lit wall panels glow the colour of flames, and are reflected in the highly-polished floor tiles and the circular, chrome bases of the furniture. The three, pod-like chairs (that are in danger of forcing their occupants into a reclining position akin to having a dental check) are a brilliant red, hot spots of colour that might fire the imagination, or engender a quick, hard sell. The small, circular lights which lie flush with the ceiling burn with a bright, white intensity. Indeed, depending on one's aesthetic sensibility and emotional stability, *Reception 1* might evoke either heaven or hell.

Reception 1 is one of five striking photographs by Peter Bobby currently on show at the Mission Gallery, Swansea. Composed of intoxicating colours and elaborate shapes, these photographs depict newly-constructed, corporate spaces in all their pristine glory: frosted glass and coloured perspex, vibrant paint-work and polished surfaces, twinkling spot-lights and creatively concealed strip-lighting. The spaces have yet to record their function in the wear and tear of the materials; one can only anticipate the stains on the soft-furnishings, the finger prints on the glass, the grease marks left on the stainless-steel. Similarly, the corporate logos and displays, the brochures and self-standing cut-outs have yet to arrive. (*Reception II* and *Reception V* reproduced in the catalogue are exceptions, however, they are not included in the Mission Gallery exhibition.) For now, only the strategically placed security cameras and smoke alarms suggest that these places are intended as anything other than show-rooms.

The Mission Gallery, a converted, nineteenth-century chapel, is relatively small. The five photographs, each measuring 165 cm x 108 cm, fill the available wall space; the curved walls of the apse are not suitable for such mammoth prints. Rather than leave the apse bare, however, Bobby has 'created specifically' a rather minimal piece of work entitled *Lift Numbers, G to 6*. It is tempting to suggest he shouldn't have bothered. For while the photographs attest to an impressive technical skill (Bobby is a highly accomplished photographer), *Lift Numbers, G to 6* depends upon a flawed and somewhat facile concept. It comprises seven images, each with a number or letter constructed out of dots (G, 1, 2, 3). Each image, then, is intended to depict the illuminated display panel (usually beside or above the lift door) that indicates the position of the elevator as it moves through the lift-shaft: up and down the building. The exhibition literature claims that by 'clinically documenting the journey of the lift's ascension, Bobby alludes to the passage of time and suggests the possibility of human presence. This gives the work a tangible sense of reality and questions what lies beyond the public facade [of corporate reception areas], a condition often absent in his other images.' I remain unconvinced. How, for instance, do some little pictures of display panels (hung in a horizontal line) provide Bobby's sumptuous photographs with 'a tangible sense of reality which is otherwise lacking? Equally, if their purpose is to infer time and human activity, surely his photographs might already and far more eloquently achieve that aim? (Remember the security cameras and the smoke alarms.) In fact, all *Lift Numbers, G to 6* succeeds in doing is to dilute, and detract from, an impressive piece of photographic work.

The same can be said for the overwrought terms in which Bobby's photographs are described. Though his photographs succeed in demonstrating the sterile chic of corporate spaces before they've been invaded by employees and customers, the ideas that apparently underpin his carefully researched and beautifully controlled images are disappointingly trite, despite the baffling jargon in which they are couched. Both Bobby and Paul Jeff (who provides the essay for the accompanying 'monograph' published by Ffotogallery and Mission Gallery) are desperate to define the reception rooms in 'negative' terms: 'non-places' and 'false edifices'. These foyers are 'alien, stark and austere' in contrast to the 'visually sensuous' photographs which derive from them. They are simultaneously the silent antithesis to the hustle and bustle of city life, and 'transitional spaces' in which each visitor is momentarily 'relieved of his usual determinants'. But the ideas seem confused and contradictory, and the arguments are obfuscatory. In fact, there remains an over-riding sense that while Bobby's photographs are truly fascinating and engaging, the highfalutin prose that is meant to validate them is not.

The spaces Bobby photographs are doubtless the result of sophisticated market research. Invariably, the multi-sensory effect of each reception area will inspire different responses in different people, but the chances are that each has been designed with a certain clientele in mind, and most probably the chosen few will respond favourably and, more significantly, knowingly. (Jeff's assertion that 'Peter Bobby shows us what we have created and we are at once amazed and aghast' implies that though the customer is always right, s/he is also rather dim.) As for the photographs, what they exquisitely reveal are the colour co-ordinated constructions of corporate space which make palatable the economic relations on which capitalism is based. But, because they are photographs (lasting monuments to transient moments), they also mournfully announce the inevitable deterioration of these unused, unspoilt receptions rooms, as the decor becomes shabby and the style passé.

Jane Fletcher

Above: *Reception 1*

Opposite above: *Reception 3*

Opposite below: *Reception 2*

digital subversions

Sharon Ya'ari was at Lisson Gallery, 14th November - 18th January

On first impression the imagery of Israeli photographer Sharon Ya'ari is a reminder of how reduced one's sense of place becomes when mediated primarily through images of conflict. The wider landscape of Israel and the events of everyday life that feature in this work take on a precious and improbable tranquility given the political context. Not that this work asserts this type of identification. The most overt reference to conflict occurs with a photograph of large tent, which may or may not be army issue. Ya'ari's photography defies established visual categorisation. In the most general of terms it undramatically documents people at their leisure, usually situated in marginal type landscapes (landscapes that are neither rural nor urban). Preferring to photograph during winter, when the light is subdued and the vegetation green, these landscapes take on a slightly European feel. It's one aspect of a more general sense that these places are slightly estranged from themselves.

In an image entitled *Iris Hill, South East View* we see families walking a popular landscape feature situated by an improbably busy road. In the far distance, residential settlements, the land in-between, a mixture of infertile looking scrub and small-scale cultivation. In another image entitled *Zoo*, a complex of tree branches partially conceals our view of a family standing before a large animal enclosure housing an emu and a gazelle-like creature. In other images teenagers are shown doing teenage type things: three girls are seen entering a derelict hide away (referred to in the title of the work as an 'old fair ground'), in another, a group of children gather behind a broken wall. Ya'ari rarely reveals the full face of his subjects. Usually disclosing only the back or the side of a person. The effect is to keep the viewer at some distance from the events depicted.

Despite the unproblematic way in which this work has been appreciated on a documentary level, their presence in the Lisson gallery (bastions of conceptual artist practice) alerts one to the improbability that this is straight documentary work. Without knowing why, a number of images don't quite make sense. Most notably a diptych entitled *Cars 2/3 Right & Cars 2/3 Left*. The left-hand side (perversely entitled *Cars 2/3 Right*) shows two cars waiting, presumably at a crossing of some kind. The right-hand image shows three cars waiting. I cannot explain why, but the image does not make sense – there is an abiding sense that something has been removed from the scene although what this could be is unclear. It should be no surprise (although few reviews of the show mentioned it) that a number of these works have been digitally manipulated – some subtly, some are composites of several images, and others may not have been altered at all. The diptych probably belongs to the latter possibility.

The range of Ya'ari's interventions resist a prescriptive deconstruction of their critical significance. The *Zoo* image for example shows the same two men twice. The trees in the foreground are probably superimposed – significantly they are framed so as not to be shown growing from the ground (the same tree may in fact figure twice, taken from different angles and having been digitally pruned). The image showing teenagers gathered behind a wall is in fact a composite of five images. Again, two of the boys appear twice from different angles. In an image taken in a place of rest for the dead, one of the chairs has five legs, another has a missing supporting strut.

It's not difficult to find a political significance for such interventions: the digital becoming just another subversion of everyday normality; the desire to multiply presences when faced with an enemy who wishes your absence; the removing of people from an image as an expression of everyday fears (one image shows a girl alone with a tombstone, in the original image a number of people stood around her).

But in part, such moves also internalise the interpretation of the photograph to the nature of the image itself and thereby posit an autonomy from context. While there is perhaps an inevitability to this work accruing political meaning it also asserts the possibility of an artistic and photographic imagination beyond the political.

Paul Tebbs

BOOK REVIEWS

SPECTRAL EVIDENCE
ALBERT BAER

ALEXEY BRODOVITCH
KERRY WILLIAM PURCELL

THE IRISH, PHOTOGRAPHY IN IRELAND, A CENTURY IN FOCUS
SEXTON, CHANDLER, MAGUIRE

ACTUAL LIFE
TOBY GLANVILLE

ENVISIONING SCIENCE
FELICE FRANKEL
OTT'S SNEEZE
NORFOLK, WHITE

HOME
LARS TUNBJÖRK

APERTURE AT 50
R.H.CRAVENS

SPECTRAL EVIDENCE
THE PHOTOGRAPHY OF TRAUMA

MIT press
£19.95
Albert Baer
ISBN: 0-262-02515-9

A simple view of time is that it passes by, rather like a flowing river. Photographs simply freeze a particular moment in the regular passage of time. After the event, they can be useful in remembering time past. They provide evidence for historians to build a narrative. However, they are meagre and opaque evidence, so theorists stress the importance of context.

Ulrich Baer rejects this whole approach. In Baer's view, neither the passage of time nor history is inherently sequential. Time is marked by events that suddenly burst and explode. Events do not so much unfold as erupt.

In addition, photographs are not frozen moments taken from (and fitting into) a continuous loop of time. In fact, photographs are images of events that may fail to be integrated. Photographs mark the end of the art of storytelling. The camera does not fracture the world so much as disclose that the world is a mass of discontinuous moments. This raises the problem of how to use photographs to recall a past that was not experienced. The Holocaust is Baer's

special concern: most people did not experience it, therefore it is literally unremembered – and yet it cannot be forgotten.

In common with many theorists, Baer does not accept that the meaning or veracity of photographs is stable but he does accept their testimony about time. Photographs declare 'here it is' or 'this once was'. Photographs offer a potent illusion of the moment but, despite its intensity, the moment does not unfold to reveal what happened 'before' and 'after'. Photographs do not parcel out time, preserving it in a world of connotation. Instead, photographs are like time itself – explosive, sudden, distinct.

In Baer's view, this makes photographs like a particular kind of experience, that of trauma. Trauma is characterized not by the event itself, which may or may not be catastrophic and may not traumatize everyone equally, but consists in the structure of the experience, one in which the event is not assimilated or integrated fully at the time into consciousness. As Baer writes, 'Because trauma blocks routine mental processes from converting an experience into memory or forgetting', it parallels the defining structure of photography, which also traps an event during its occurrence while blocking its transformation into memory.

There is a definite and similar paradox in both trauma and photography: the most direct representation of an event may occur as an

absolute inability to know it. Both trauma and photography are similar in these respects too: they are both later than the event itself; they are both subject to repetitive seeing; they both challenge conventional understanding of how reference works, because 'seeing' does not translate immediately into 'knowing'. Baer writes, 'Photography and trauma dispel the illusory certainty that what is seen is what can be known'.

Baer argues that what photographs show may not have been registered by the subject; what they point out may not have been fully experienced. His first example is the work of the French neurologist Jean-Martin Charcot, who reigned over thousands of hysterical women and men in his hospital in Paris in the 1870-80s. He used photographs to capture experiences that had never entered memory in the first place. He used flash to separate the women from their world and intended to control their experiences in ways they could not do for themselves. But he recorded more than he bargained for – the women look back at us. Baer suggests how we for the first time may be able to see images of victimhood from positions that break with the photographer's perspective of mastery. In other words, the women live on, and they live 'outside' Charcot.

In chapter 2 Baer analyses an image of the site of a Nazi extermination camp in Poland by Dirk Reinartz from his 1995 collection *Deathly Still: Pictures of Former Concentration Camps*. The picture shows a clearing in a woodland, but the viewer is unable to see a recognisable 'place'. There is nothing that points directly to the 'Holocaust'. Baer also analyses an image from Mikael Levin's *War Story* (1997), which depicts the former concentration camp of Ohrdruf in Germany. The photograph rejects the aesthetics of 'landscape' for a flat abstraction, turning depth into uninhabitable 'terrain'. Levin, like Reinartz, forces us to see that there is nothing to see. Their images arrive at a symbolic and conceptual 'grey zone', where looking is more like blank staring. In these photographs absence does not become a meaningful 'Nothingness' but a useless voiding of reference, with no significance at all. They show a devastation that prevents interpretation from 'outside': 'The disaster ruins everything, all the while leaving everything intact'.

Baer's final chapter focuses on a set of coloured slides taken in the Lodz ghetto between 1942-44 by Walter Genewein, a Nazi accountant. These photographs attempt to install the ghetto as a model labour site. However, Darius Jablonski's documentary film *Fotoamator* (1998) uses Genewein's slides and creates the illusion that the Jews have been released. In other words, Jablonski gives them a future. In so doing, argues Baer, photographs can become an open-ended form of testimony to the history of how a person lives on 'outside' Genewein's Nazi gaze. Baer insists we acknowledge that photography 'gives refuge' to a time that is 'unredeemed', or undefined and unknown.

Baer is antagonistic to those 'melancholic' theorists (such as Barthes, and Cadava) who discuss photographs as metaphors for the cemetery, the grave and the crypt. He is driven by the photograph's capacity to serve as 'the rearguard of memory that defends 'against oblivion, against death'. That is the value of the relation between photographs and trauma. Every photograph stages the breakdown of context that is its structural analogy to trauma. There can be

no recourse to the historians, searching for narrative completeness. Instead, memory must derive from images that reveal experiences that have not been, and possibly cannot be, assimilated in such a continuous narrative. Critically, the images he considers 'stage not a return of the real but its first appearance'. Like trauma, they stage that which is unremembered but yet that which cannot be forgotten. Baer considers that we are 'responsible for the first time for a past moment that has been blasted out of time'. We have to find 21st century methods to question the Nazi perspective recorded in all their documents, and work against their aim to equate Jewish existence with death and non-existence. For Benjamin's admonition still holds good: 'Even the dead will not be safe from the enemy if he wins'.

John Taylor

ALEXEY BRODOVITCH

Phaidon Press
£45.00
Kerry William Purcell
ISBN: 071841633

Advanced photographic theory has rightly insisted that images depend a great deal for their meaning on text and context. Yet too often it fails to engage meaningfully with the history and practice of graphic design. Similarly, graphic design tends to ignore the many insights of photo theory. There have been several connected reasons for this: photo theory still prefers the purity of the photographic image (as do the discourses of art to which they tend to gravitate). Secondly, the mobility of the photograph – its capacity to reappear in different cultural spaces – makes the page recede over time from photographic culture. Plus, the elevation of photography as a serious subject has led to an overlooking of the domains of the applied and commercial image.

Aside from the important accounts of the Bauhaus, of the political avant-gardes of the 1920s and the odd discussion of advertising and photojournalism, photo theory has turned a blind eye to the page as a primary site. It has given a false picture of how photographs actually work and of how the vast majority of photographers work intimately with (or as) designers, writers and editors. This is deeply contradictory given that all but a few of the world's photographs are seen in print and that contemporary photography is now so deeply embedded in visual design culture.

Although it doesn't set out directly to redress any of this, Kerry William Purcell's study of the work of Alexey Brodovitch is highly illuminating. Brodovitch was an illustrator, typographer, occasional photographer, art director and graphic designer. His impact on graphic and photographic practice was enormous during a career that began in Europe in the 1920s and flourished in North America in the following decades. He is most widely known for his years as art director of *Harper's Bazaar* with its glamorous synthesis of fashion editorials and high-life profiles. However Purcell's book focuses equally on Brodovitch as a champion of the practices of others and a collaborator who developed a highly nuanced understanding of the page as a space of creative and critical interaction.

Brodovitch produced only one book of his own photographs. The groundbreaking *Ballet* (1945) was one of the first attempts to fully exploit motion blur, shallow focus and errant exposure within an expressive documentary book. More significantly he was pivotal to the careers of many other photographers including Irving Penn, Richard Avedon, Hans Namuth and Lillian Bassman. Not only did he work closely with image-makers on commercial projects, he ran a highly influential series of classes and workshops, the Design Laboratory based at the University of Pennsylvania.

André Kertész benefited from several commissions from Brodovitch, and was assisted in the publication and design of his first book *Day of Paris* (1945). The now classical layout was a simple yet highly modulated use of word and image, saving the graphic flair for the book's jacket which wrapped its title around the walls of a building on a street corner. The book *Observations* (1959), billed as a collaboration between Richard Avedon and the writer Truman Capote was really a three-hander, intelligently designed by Brodovitch using his skills developed in magazine work.

Brodovitch's subtle grasp of the relation between graphics and photographics was equally well demonstrated in a feature in *Harper's Bazaar* (October 1952). Henri Cartier-Bresson generally insisted on full frame reproduction of his photographs (an instance of an emerging defence of photographers against insensitive designers). Brodovitch showed him two layouts of his pictures using uncropped and then cropped images, the latter meeting the photographer's rare approval in the context of the overall design.

The visual approach of Brodovitch was spacious and meticulous, informed by a precise sense of scale and proportion. This lent itself perfectly to the aspirant consumer culture of *Harper's* post war readership. But it was also a generous approach that could accommodate the work of others. This is perhaps why his most assured and ambitious success was the short-lived magazine *Portfolio*. Running for just three issues in 1950 and 1951 it aimed to be a showcase for the best in contemporary art and design. Each issue comprised a series of discrete multi-page folios. The diverse subjects included the photography of Cartier-Bresson, Irving Penn and Richard Avedon, stereoscopy, commercial illustration, graffiti, cattle brands, product design, xerography (early photocopying), typography, book design and student projects. While the magazine had a visual consistency it was never at odds with the variety material it presented. For this *Portfolio* is still

highly regarded by contemporary designers. Brodovitch was a stylish formalist certainly, but this kind of formalism contains a radical potential because within it there lays a disregard for accepted distinctions between high culture and low, the conservative and the progressive, the mainstream and the avant-garde. In this sense his work heralds the best and the worst tendencies of our postmodern culture.

For all its initial democracy printed matter soon goes out of circulation and becomes almost inaccessible, taking a central aspect of photography's cultural history with it. (The same is happening with the self-erasing culture of internet web design, which is only now beginning to be archived by museums and libraries.) Besides its engaging account of the working life of Brodovitch, a real strength of Purcell's book is the decision to devote many of its pages to the reproduction of his important publications. *Ballet*, *Day of Paris*, *Observations* and the three issues of *Portfolio*, all well out of print now, are presented in their entirety as grids of photo/graphic spreads. This device is common to other recent publications such as *Fotografia Publica: Photography in Print 1919-1939* (1999) and *The Book of 101 Books: Seminal Photographic Books of the Twentieth Century* (2001), both of which contain work by Brodovitch. Purcell's *Alexey Brodovitch* joins them as one of a number of books that are beginning slowly to assemble the missing history of the photographic page.

David Campany

THE IRISH

A Photo History 1840-1940
Thames and Hudson
£24.95
Sean Sexton and Christine Kinealy
ISBN: 0500 510070

PHOTOGRAPHY IN IRELAND

The Nineteenth Century
Edmund Burke
£45.00
Edward Chandler
ISBN: 0946130345

A CENTURY IN FOCUS

Photography and Photographers in the North of Ireland 1839-1939
Blackstaff Press
£20.00
W.A. Maguire
ISBN: 0-85640-679-1

Objecting to subject matter as the only criterion of evaluation in publications of early Irish photography, Edward Chandler, in the introduction to his *Photography in Ireland*, suggests that what is ignored by subject orientated histories of photography are those other criteria that photographic historians also find important; composition, print quality, pictorial value and the 'creator' of the image. These are qualifying methods employed in histories of the photographic image, however, they tend to be matters of historicism rather than evaluative criteria. Composition, print and pictorial quality, are not eternal values that simply materialised in the chemical ether that helped give birth to the first photographic image. They emerged out of a lexicon that described, conceptualised and defined aspects of particular practices of image making. Frequently merging with other evaluative criteria at different historical junctions, this lexicon became the means to differentiate divergent photographic practices.

Chandler clearly positions his history of Irish photography within these other criteria, yet nowhere does he outline a framework for the evaluative judgements that he identifies as being important other than his statement that they

exist. Apart from a brief discussion on the influence of romantic and pastoral allegory on Irish amateur art photography there is no insight into the criteria Chandler employs in deciding pictorial quality. One could assume however, that it is from the position of the collector rather than the historian, that Chandler's qualifying judgements are made.

The book's opening section is a chronologically ordered survey of forty-four photographic images from 1839-1900. The high production value reproductions are examples of the work of exemplary Irish photographers chosen in the words of Chandler 'not only for their fine photographic qualities but also because of interesting subject matter.' Chandler obviously takes great pleasure in his role as collector, the eye of connoisseurship not only frames his choice of images in the plate section but also drives his historical narrative of Irish photography. Much of the book is caught up in establishing the provenance of specific images.

The criteria that seems to be most pressing for Chandler is the 'creator' of the image and he has carried out extensive research to establish the prominence of specific individuals in the development of Irish photography. Chandler's history is thus very much a canon, a chronologically ordered list of significant Irish photographers and photographs. Pre-eminent among these is Leone Gluckman who established a Daguerreotype studio in Dublin in the mid 1840's. Gluckman, who spuriously gave himself the title Professor of Natural Philosophy not only ran a daguerreotype studio but also conducted an electric light demonstration from Nelson's Pillar as part of the illuminations to commemorate Queen Victoria's visit to Dublin in 1849 and opened a Museum of Anatomy, Science and Art in 1863. Gluckman's conflated interest in art, technology and the medical sciences emerged from the Enlightenment culture of modernity. However, Chandler does not elaborate on the convergence between Gluckman's varied interest in the sciences the careers of all three are covered in one brief chapter. Many of the photographs reproduced in Maguire's history are drawn from the collections of the Ulster Museum and the Ulster Folk and Transport Museum which house some of the most significant ethnographic photographic collections of late 19th and early 20th century Ireland.

Chandler's comments on subject orientated publications of early Irish photography could be read in many ways as a slight on Sean Sexton's *The Irish: A Photo History*. Unlike Chandler and Maguire Sexton's publication is not a history of photography but photography of history, the images reproduced here are chosen largely on the basis of subject matter rather than any aesthetic criteria. The images are framed by Christine Kinealy's historical narrative covering 19th century landownership and famine to 1916, the Civil War and the modernisation of post-partition Ireland.

There is a paradox in the relationship between Kinealy's text and the photographs reproduced in this book. It is clear from the introduction that the author considers photographs historical documents, containing within one rectangular frame the simultaneous and seemingly limitless existence of information on its subject. They are empirical evidence, a footnote to Kinealy's overarching narrative of Irish history. However, photography like history has a rhetoric, and the rhetoric of Kinealy's text is clear, there is no revisionism in this account of Irish history. Photographs are shot through and through with ideology; the choice of vantage point, camera angle and subject matter all contribute to how the subjects of photographs are read. Just as there is a historical discourse, a way of writing and speaking about history, there is a photographic discourse. The discourse of photography often merges with other discourses, photography becomes embedded in the activities and processes that shape history. This often gets lost in the treatment of photographs as facts. It is not just a matter of reading photographs against the backdrop of

and arts.

Like Chandler, W.A. Maguire in *A Century in Focus* includes a lengthy appendix of commercial photographers in his history of photography in the North of Ireland. Indeed both books contain important reference material on the commercial development of photography throughout the nineteenth century. However, Maguire is less concerned with amateur gentlemen photographers than Chandler, his chapter on this subject concentrating on those professional photographers who participated in various work orientated leisure

activities such as natural history, ethnography and geology.

Taking a broad sweep across photography in Northern Ireland, the chapters cover large chronological periods of technological evolution, popular genres and the careers of photographers. This results in the omission of specific photographic activities in favour of a general overview of photographic practices. The involvement of R.J. Welch, Alexander Hogg and William Green in the photographic activities of The Belfast Naturalists Field Club is a book in itself yet history or as frozen slices of historical time; photographic practices need to be read as emerging out of and within historical processes.

The difficulty in simply treating photographs as facts is evident in the first two chapters dealing with the landlordism, famine and poverty. Much of Kinealy's text in these chapters revolves around what was not photographed. It is as if the historian is searching through the remnants of historical documentation for visual proof of an event. Yet the images do tell us something about the visual practices of colonialism. The photographs of the landlords' demesne and the tenants plot speak of a different organisation of pictorial space. An image such as Robert French's photograph of Lismore Castle is a property-scape, land that has been aestheticised according to the visual regime of the picturesque. A practice that not only made the colonised space visually familiar to the mobile gaze of the coloniser but also removed any trace of the indigenous populations relationship to the land. The pictorial space of a tenants cottage at Connemara however is that colonial space that is not supposed to be viewed, in John Barrell's terms it is the dark side of the landscape, laboured land not worthy of the colonial gaze. It is by exploring the relationship and tensions between this imagery rather than examining them as separate entities that the visual evidence that Kinealy appears to be seeking may be found.

It is the role of photography within the visual practices of colonialism rather than simply representations of it that photography is useful as history, Chandler may well be right in his complaint that subject orientated histories ignore other more aesthetic concerns, yet these too need to be located historically. Pictorial, print and aesthetic quality emerged out of history they should not simply be mapped onto it from the vantage point of the present.

Justin Carville

ACTUAL LIFE

Toby Glanville
£16.95
Photoworks
ISBN: 1-903796-06-7

Photoworks have been commissioning photographers to work on projects in the south east of England for some years now. The benefits of this rootedness have never been better exemplified than in this book of photographs by Toby Glanville taken over three years and starting from two Kent villages, Westerham and Goudhurst. The title, *Actual Life*, suggests that there is a polemic concealed behind the gentle face of these pictures (the majority of which are portraits) and looking at the locations of some of the photographs – Shoreham, Ashford – you realise that these names have become familiar as the stage for a national debate about asylum seekers. Does the title therefore set the book against a media representation of Kent? Or perhaps *Actual Life* is rather making a claim for the documentary power of photographs to bring us into contact with people's lives?

One of the portraits shows Richard, an employee of Tesco's, information we discover from his name badge. But elsewhere in the book the emphasis is on an older way of life, be it churches, a high street butcher or a man tending old cars in a garage. There are many pictures of people over 60 or younger than 20 but not very much in between. Kent is now part of the commuter belt for London but there are no thrusting young professionals (presumably all at work) only a woman creating, or more likely restoring, stained glass. There is also a picture of a rose, meadows and a garden bonfire. Before long this adds up to a lexicon of semi-rural Englishness of a kind now more familiar, with the colour turned up, from Martin Parr photographs.

Alongside these pictures are a number of photographs taken in schools, giving small institutional details of the kitchens and dining halls. They suggest order, a well bedded down security and will provoke a faint nostalgia for departed youth on the part of anyone who attended such a school.

In 1998 when this project was in progress the Photoworks magazine *Insight* reported that Glanville was 'working with local people, their histories and the shifting cultural identity of one of Britain's agricultural heartlands.' Only it appears that their cultural identity has not shifted very much beyond the clothes they are wearing. Otherwise there is a decidedly 19th century feel about these pictures.

In both his documenting of a particular area and in the manner in which he has photographed people living a life that seems as yet untouched by mobile phones and computers, Glanville is like a latter day Emerson capturing a world soon to disappear (or which has already gone). And to extend the 19th century comparison there are a few pictures that are decidedly pre-Raphaelite in their aesthetic. In particular a double portrait of two girls sitting in front of a church, one, judging by her gaze unable to see, recalls a painting by Millais, *The Blind Girl*. This extends not only to the pathos of being subject matter but also to the tree blossom scattered on the

grass (a rainbow in the painting serves the same function) and the implied religiousity of the position in front of a church.

By this stage I may have given the impression that this book is irredeemably backward looking and sentimental but this is not the case. *Actual Life* may present a partial view of a Kent that has not changed very much in the last 50 years but the photographer's engagement with his subject is nevertheless frank and serious.

In his portraits of children Glanville finds a strand that unifies an unchanged way of life and the contemporary world coming into formation. His portrait of two boys standing by a fence manages to be both suggestive of 18th century swagger and schoolboy anxieties. Adam Phillips in his introduction writes about the way children are 'deciding who and how to be' when photographed, or 'experimenting with boldness' and the pictures demonstrate a very subtle edginess on the part of children trying to discover how they can present themselves to the camera. This investigaton of individual identity adds a counterpoint to the static cultural identity elsewhere in the photographs. If not exactly 'actual life' the book discovers enough rich individual encounters to recommend it to many readers.

HOME

Lars Tunbjörk
£20.00
Steidl
ISBN: 3-88243-868-1

Lars Tunbjörk's last monograph *Office* documented the expression of the personal within the sterile uniformity of corporate working environments. *Home* by contrast, documents the relative absence of the personal where the personal could be expected to reside and flourish – within and around the home. Returning to the places he grew up in (many are taken in Stockholm), *Home* records a vague sense of disconnection from the once familiar. A sensation recognisable to any who return to the places of their past. Despite the biographical pretext however, there is little imperative to imagine the significance of these locations in terms of an individual life. Drama of any kind, let alone the topology of a boy's rites of passage, are entirely absent from this work.

The book's cover image shows a blanched vision of houses (built to an identical design) receding into the distance. It verges on the nostalgic – the underexposed image aping something of a recollection's lost fidelity. If it wasn't for the leafless sapling and newly flowering tulips occupying the foreground space one might think of summer. But both the feel and aesthetic of this image are unrepresentative of the publication as a whole. It seems to allude to an alternative relation to the locations documented that is not manifest between the book's covers. Tunbjörk's aesthetic is closely related to photography's paradoxical, but seemingly *de rigueur*, alienated mode of visual appreciation – a redemptive formalism proffered to the overlooked and the underloved things of this world by a disengaged proxy of a subjectivity. It's a critical mode softened by Tunbjörk's hovering familiarity with his locale. It's a mode that lapses altogether

with incongruous intimacies with plant-life (some beautiful blooms, others blunt ground configurations of marigolds and begonias encircled by concrete) and unenlightening confrontations with dumb domestic objects (plastic moulds, cheap grey carpet and soap). The majority of these images were however taken outside, often under a clear blue sky, looking onto houses and their gardens from a threshold (a doorway, driveway or a fence) – but with little sense of exclusion or surreptitiousness.

Since the late 1980s Tunbjörk has been critically examining the notion of 'Swedishness' (most notably in *Country Beside Itself: Pictures of Sweden*) and *Home* necessarily shadows this project. And the nuances of the polemic internalised in this work may be closed to those unfamiliar with the social and political identity of the country. A politics, which in recent years, has moved marginally away from high taxation and prodigious social welfare provision to a more individualistic political ideology and, in common with many European countries, has seen increased support for the political right.

Only three people appear in this book (there are 50 images in total), two of them, incidental background occurrences. It's an absence that encourages one to seek something of their identity in the landscape, but it also allows the broad socio-political and economic forces that have sculpted these locations to emerge. The houses are generally remarkable for their unremarkableness – practical orderliness without preciousness. If equating the British with their homes is an imperfect but potentially informative game, in Sweden, from my perspective at least, it reveals nothing. No face is given in this book and no face was imagined.

The short introduction to *Home* suggests it is about 'quietness', about there being 'nothing conspicuous', about the 'same as ever', 'a neutral zone with no obvious reason to worry'. But one senses that it would be wrong to assume these

Richard West

qualities are being celebrated. In one image towards the conclusion of the book, two national flags hang limply in the shadows at identical heights from two identical homes. The overwhelming feeling is of vapidness.

Paul Tebbs

ENVISIONING SCIENCE
The Design and Craft of the Science Image

£36.95

Felice Frankel

MIT Press

ISBN: 0-262-06225-9

OTT'S SNEEZE

£9.95

Bookworks

Lawrence Norfolk and Neal White

ISBN: 870699 52 1

While the telescope enables us to see a system in every star, the microscope unfolds to us a world in every universe'

The Microscope and its Wonders, 1866

'On January 7, Frederic P. Ott stood before the world's first movie camera and sneezed. But the droplets and globules expelled by Ott were too fast, too small or too many for the primitive camera to record. The sneeze recorded here is the one the camera did not see'

Norfolk and White

Norfolk and White tell us that they have recreated a historical moment: the first motion picture to be copyrighted in the United States. What they do, of course, using the latest laser and computer technology to capture the droplets and globules, to visually record what was invisible to the more 'primitive' Kinetograph invented by Edison, is to create what they think a record of a sneeze should be.

The fascination of capturing the invisible on film, whether photographic or cinematic lies at the heart of both books. The narrative that is suggested, however, is that what we see here is

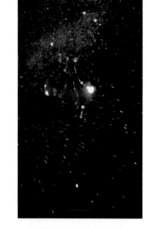

merely the subvisible – what has always been there but remained beneath the threshold of human vision until the latest technological invention. But inventions are always social before they are technical and in this review I argue for a more historically grounded understanding of scientific visual technologies, rather than a narrative of technological progress.

Neal and White's work is a kind of art flick book; it includes the original images of Ott's facial expression caught in 45 frames and contrasts this with a kind of cosmic revelation of the sneeze itself, now separated from the body (in this case White's). Here the abstract images suggest nothing less than a night sky filled with clusters of stars (as the authors state, along with the possibility of 'high altitude footage of fire-bombing of Dresden'). This is not incidental. Historically, the telescope and microscope, inventions of the 17th century, promised to reveal in macro and microcosm 'other worlds', the infinite and infinitesimal, through which man might travel.

Microscopes however, had one advantage over telescopes. Unlike the divinely created and immutable solar system which man had to look up to (and merely confirmed his insignificance), the microcosmic universe might be brought within the orbit of a god-like observer who now literally looked down the tube of a microscope. And while man could not hope to touch the former, the latter, in time, offered scope for manipulation.

With the invention of photography and film in the nineteenth century microscopy acquired a singular power. As Giuliana Bruno has suggested, it is too easily forgotten that photography and film are discourses which share 'epistemological foundations with scientific investigation'. They are detailing techniques in the etymological sense of the verb *détailler*: to cut in pieces.

Until recently such histories have been repressed in favour of a history of photography and film as arts. Photomicrography has largely been ignored within the history of photography; the Lumiére brothers shift to medical research and production has largely been ignored. Detailed visual information was, and remains, crucial to the rise of the sciences and consequently there was an explosion of microscopic media in the nineteenth century. The result of this was that 'any significant qualitative difference between a biosphere and a mechanosphere began to evaporate' (Crary: 1995). Significantly, *Envisioning Science* includes both computer components and cellular examples thus emphasising their connection.

However, I want to move a little further back from the images displayed here in order to think about the body of the observer-photographer, the subject, and the object that is photographed. In short, I want to think about what is left out of the picture.

Microscopes are now neither portable nor hand-held. They are fixed and the observer must come to them and be harnessed as a component in the machinery. *Envisioning Science* lacks this information, or indeed about the complex procedure for preparing cellular specimens in the first place. The process begins, as Rob Stepney describes, by 'taking tissue representative of the feature under study, and fixing it (often in formalin) to prevent putrefaction and degeneration. The sample is then placed in increasing concentrations of alcohol to remove all water. Once dehydration is complete, the alcohol is removed by immersion in an organic solvent... the next stage is to embed the tissue in a medium that provides strength and support. In light microscopy, it is usual to impregnate the specimen with paraffin wax. The solidified block of tissue is then cut by a microtome. This machine shave off a series of sections, each around 4-5 micrometres thick, forming a ribbon of samples. The ribbon is floated in water, and sections picked up on a glass microscope slide, ready to be dried and stained'.

Staining is important because most cells are transparent and therefore without staining there would literally be nothing to see. Stepney tells us that 'the history of science is as much one of improved straining techniques as of improved microscopes.' Only then is the image 'taken' and printed. I leave aside processes of 'cleaning' without losing what Frankel call 'integrity' and the various different types of microscopes employed.

The point is that the photographic print, whether analogue or digital, is the outcome of a complex and lengthy process of labour often involving a number of people. Latour describes such an image as merely 'the fine edge and final stage' of this whole process. Its function is to 'modify the scale of the rhetoric.' That is, without widespread publication and accelerated circulation, without a wide viewing public, the image is worthless.

But it is not only a naïve viewing public whose perception is shaped by such images. Latour has also argued that 'scientists start seeing something once they stop looking at nature and look exclusively and obsessively at prints and flat inscriptions... in the debates around perception, what is always forgotten is this simple drift from watching confusing three-dimensional objects to inspecting two-dimensional images which have been made less confusing.' This would seem to be borne out in the advice Frankel gives the photographer: 'simply put, simplify your image ...the simpler the image, the more accessible and engaging it becomes – because there is less to figure out.'

In both books, and in gazing at these beautiful, abstract patterns, whether in black and white or in stained, saturated, fluorescent colour, the viewer is not encouraged to 'figure out' anything at all. Like twinkling stars, the images dazzle; we become lost, absorbed in magnificent detail. Indeed, all we are asked to do is marvel at the wonders of modern science in providing us with so much to see (yet so little to know). We should resist being absorbed into the image and work a little harder at figuring out for ourselves how we come to know what we see.

Roberta McGrath

PHOTOGRAPHY PAST FORWARD
APERTURE AT 50

Thames and Hudson
£29.95
R.H.Cravens
ISBN: 0500 283974

Recently we witnessed several anthologies based on photography magazines – among them *Camerawork*, *Photofile* and *Creative Camera*, the latter edited and introduced by myself. The latest title to repackage itself is *Aperture*, which marks its 50th birthday with a book that is bigger, glossier and more self-confident than anything so far.

In the league of photography titles *Aperture* occupies a legendary position – founded, no less, by the disciples of Stieglitz himself, the magazine was conceived as the successor of *Camera Work*. After Stieglitz closed his journal and 291 gallery in 1917, modern photography lacked a forum and a powerful advocate. Its masters dead or ailing (like Weston) or exiled (like Strand), the movement would need to wait for end of the war before it regrouped with new blood to lobby anew for photography.

Part of the *Aperture* legend involves its symbolic origins in 1952. These are described in part one of a four-part history written by R.H. Cravens that gathers together the thematic threads that span the decades. Aperture was conceived during a high-spirited conference of photographers attended by representatives of the old guard, including Ansel Adams and Barbara Morgan, and including young Turks fresh from military service, such as Minor White and Beaumont Newhall. Stieglitz, who had died six years earlier, was a 'spectre ... present among the *Aperture* founders that day in 1952 [as] an indelible personality and an elusive ideal,' writes Cravens.

The quarterly was launched with an ethos that borrowed heavily from Stieglitz's concept of 'equivalents' (wherein the iconicity of the image transcends its index, transforming the image from

a representation into a revelation of the inner emotions of the artist). It was charged with being the standard of the movement. Issue one contained a manifesto that committed the publication to be platform for the works of 'master' photographers, which are the 'ultimate expression' of their philosophy. For the first decade and a half *Aperture's* editor, Minor White ran it, unpaid, with help from countless volunteers and supporters who hoped that posterity would reward them. Loping from one financial crisis to the next, White kept the magazine alive. To the dismay of some board members, he used it to pursue his own agenda. (Adams's biographer describes how Adams soon resigned in frustration with White's theorising.)

Cravens' writing is at its best when describing the personalities behind the magazine, their conflicts and camaraderie. Around the time of the second closure crisis within a decade, in 1964, Michael E. Hoffman enters the scene. A rich kid with a 'prodigious skill for making a deal', Hoffman emerges as part cultural stalker, part visionary. He made it his business to become indispensable – first to White, from whom he learned editor's skills – then to many others that he needed to keep *Aperture* alive. His partnership with White began after Hoffman experienced some sort of epiphany at one of former's famous photography workshops. A counter-culture figure, par excellence and self-styled mystic, White would apparently ban the use of certain words (like, dislike, good, bad, right, wrong, interesting and should). He infuriated students with baffling exercises – such as forcing them to 'be' for long periods while standing still at a busy intersection. Craven has many anecdotes that vividly evoke the madness and abandon of these early years. The curator, Peter Bunnell remembers his internship at *Aperture*. 'Minor and the people around him really believed that if you sat down for an hour and looked at a great photograph such as Weston's *Pepper No. 30*... you'd be changed, and you'd be changed for the better...' Hoffman recalls that he used to have near 'out of body experiences' working with White on picture sequences.

An irritating flaw with Cravens' writing is that it is vague on chronology and has a tendency to use quotes without attributing them. It is implied that Hoffman edited his first issue in 1965 and it was a Weston monograph. But it is not exactly clear when, or if, White resigned as editor and when Hoffman assumed full control. I assume Carole Kismaric become editor in 1977, but again it is not certain. It would have been fascinating, and useful if the book had listed editors with their dates.

Plainly Cravens respected and admired Hoffman who he portrays as photography's Saul, converted on the highway to a calling worthy of a saint. Hoffman comes out as driven, egotistical, temperamental yet altruistic. Hoffman is credited with rescuing Aperture on many occasions – first by sweet-talking Strand's widow into donating 400 of the great man's prints to the foundation, then by masterminding the strategy of synergy by which sales from Aperture's books helped shore up the periodical's shaky finances. For all these reasons this book is and should be a tribute to Hoffman, but it is also his memorial – for he died a few months short of Aperture's 50th anniversary, the last of a generation of passionate defenders of photography and the Kane of photographic periodicals.

Hoffman kept faith with the notion of an 'enduring ideal' well after the salad days of modernism, even after he had devolved editorship to a succession of youngsters. This faith, argues Cravens, ensured that the periodical had a reasonably consistent identity throughout most of its history. What did this ideal mean to him? When pressed Hoffman would invoke the fuzzy notion of equivalence and say that, like Stieglitz, the magazine was trying 'to come into contact with a cosmic order, or a harmony'. Cravens conceded that the ideal was 'never articulated to anyone's intellectual satisfaction, but manifests in the artists and their work.'

Cravens' history is a stirring yarn of great men in extraordinary times and evokes the sense of Aperture as a convivial 'family' or 'community'. But if you are looking for indications of Aperture's stance in relation to some of the big debates of its times, then you will be disappointed. At one point Cravens ventures that what made Aperture radical in the 50s – its experiments with text and image sequences, its pioneering portfolios of master photographers – rendered it an anachronism in the 60s and 70s. But amazingly, Aperture's response to critiques and broadsides by Sontag, Burgin and others goes unrecorded.

Aside from Cravens' reverential history, the only other textual testimony is a series of short quotes to offer a 'flavour' of articles past. What a waste. On the covers a mosaic of inside spreads from old and recent issues testifies to a breadth and ambition of coverage, and shifts in modes of presentation, that hint at the complex identity of Aperture. Photography Past Forward: Aperture at 50 is essentially a bumper picture book of 250-odd illustrations, culled from back issues. Pictures from contrasting discursive spaces are combined, nicely effacing challenges to the notion of a universality of 'artistic' photography (a Larry Towell documentary image of Middle Eastern conflict faces a painting by Richter of a photograph; a Kruger text/image montage faces a digital 'documentation' by Pedro Meyer, and so on). So the play of images reinforces continuity and underplays several decades of contestation around the ontology and historiography of the photograph in/as art. This impression gives credence to Cravens' portrait of Aperture as an insular institution – chained to the impossible ideals and riteousness of an earlier generation.

Aperture's enviable reputation was always in inverse proportion to its visibility. The book tries but fails to redress this – ironically because the editors obeyed a founding ethos that ranked photographs above text in order of importance. The photographs reproduced here were plucked from their sequences. They are over familiar and add absolutely nothing to our understanding of the publication (it is not even clear which of them were published first in Aperture). By contrast, the absent historical, critical and polemical texts from Aperture are not so familiar. I am sure that our understanding of Aperture's contributions could have been greatly enhanced if more space had been given over to a careful selection of texts. Photography Past Forward: Aperture at 50 functions much better as shiny monument to its longest serving editors than as the sign of a legendary periodical.

David Brittain

CONTRIBUTORS

Paul Tebbs is a writer based in London.

John Taylor is Senior Lecturer in the History of Art and Design at Manchester Metropolitan University.

David Brittain is the former editor of Dpict.

Justin Carville teaches Historical and Theoretical Studies in Photography at Dun Laoghaire Institute of Art, Design and Technology.

Richard West is a Source editor.

Alicia Miller is the Head of Education and Public Events at the Whitechapel Art Gallery and a freelance writer living in London.

Jane Fletcher is a writer based in the West Midlands.

Roy Exley is a writer based in Sussex.

Martin Murray is a Lecturer in Critical and Cultural Theory at London Metropolitan University.

David Campany is a Senior Lecturer in the History & Theory of Photography at Surrey Institute of Art & Design.

Roberta McGrath is a part time lecturer at Napier University, Edinburgh.

Mark Durden is Reader in the History and Theory of Photography at the University of Derby.

Pete James is not a librarian. He is however, Head of Photographs at Birmingham Central Library.

Andrew Robinson is a photographer and lecturer based in Buxton, Derbyshire.

Sam Coates is Lead Artist at Sony Computer Entertainment Europe.

Tobias Zielony is a recent graduate of University of Wales College, Newport.

Clayton Irwin lives in Deptford, south-east London.

Stephen McCoy is a photographer based in Liverpool.